Study Guide for the Science Constructed-Response Tests

► ► ► ► ► ► ► ► ► ► ► ►

A PUBLICATION OF EDUCATIONAL TESTING SERVICE

Table of Contents
Study Guide for the Science Constructed-Response Tests

▶　　▶　　▶　　▶　　▶　　▶　　▶　　▶　　▶　　▶　　▶　　▶

TABLE OF CONTENTS

Chapter 1

Introduction to the Science Constructed-Response Tests and
Suggestions for Using This Study Guide   1

Chapter 2

Background Information on The Praxis Series™ Assessments   7

Chapter 3

Succeeding on the Science Content Essays Tests   11

Chapter 4

Preparing for the Science Content Essays Tests   17

Chapter 5

Practice Questions—Science Content Essays Tests   29

Chapter 6

Sample Responses and How They Were Scored—Science Content Essays Tests   55

Chapter 7

Succeeding on the Science Pedagogy Tests   79

Chapter 8

Preparing for the Science Pedagogy Tests   91

Chapter 9

Practice Questions—Science Pedagogy Tests   105

Chapter 10

Sample Responses and How They Were Scored—Science Pedagogy Tests   119

Chapter 11

Are You Ready? Last-Minute Suggestions   149

Appendix A

Study Plan Sheet   153

Appendix B

For More Information   155

Chapter 1

Introduction to the Science Constructed-Response Tests
and Suggestions for Using This Study Guide

▶ ▶ ▶ ▶ ▶ ▶ ▶ ▶ ▶ ▶ ▶ ▶

Introduction to the Science Constructed-Response Tests

The science constructed-response tests are designed for prospective secondary science teachers. The tests are designed to reflect current standards for knowledge, skills, and abilities in science education. Educational Testing Service (ETS) works in collaboration with teacher educators, higher education content specialists, and accomplished practicing teachers in the field of science education to keep the tests updated and representative of current standards.

This guide covers six different science constructed-response tests. In constructed-response tests, you are asked to answer a question or group of questions by writing out your response. It is not accurate to call constructed-response tests essay tests, because your response will not be graded on the basis of how it succeeds as an essay. Instead, your constructed response will be graded on the basis of how well it demonstrates an understanding of the principles of science and their appropriate application.

This guide covers the following tests, all of which are one hour long:

Test Name	Code	Number and Format of Questions
Biology: Content Essays	0233	Three multipart questions, one each on cellular and molecular biology, genetics and evolution, and organismal biology and ecology Skills and/or competencies to be tested include understanding concepts, models, and systems; analyzing data and designing investigations; understanding relationships of science, technology, and society.
Chemistry: Content Essays	0242	Three constructed-response questions on structure/property correlations and chemical reactions Skills and/or competencies to be tested include understanding concepts, models, and systems; analyzing data and designing investigations; understanding relationships of science, technology, and society.
Physics: Content Essays	0262	Three constructed-response questions on matter and energy and fields and waves Skills and/or competencies to be tested include understanding concepts, models, and systems; analyzing data and designing investigations; understanding relationships of science, technology, and society.

Test Name	Code	Number and Format of Questions
General Science: Content Essays	0433	Three multipart questions, one each on physical science, life science, and earth-space science Skills and/or competencies to be tested include understanding concepts, models, and systems; analyzing data and designing investigations; understanding relationships of science, technology, and society.
Life Science: Pedagogy	0234	One three-part constructed-response question on lesson design, strategies of instruction, and techniques of assessment and evaluation.
Physical Science: Pedagogy	0483	One multipart constructed-response question on learning objectives, strategies of instruction, methods of assessment and evaluation, and a follow-up lesson.

How to Use This Book

This book gives you instruction, practice, and test-taking tips to help you prepare for taking the science constructed-response tests. In chapter 2 you will find a discussion of The Praxis Series™—what it is and how the tests are developed. If you plan to take a Science Content Essays test, you should turn to chapters 3, 4, 5, and 6; if you plan to take a Science Pedagogy test, you should turn to chapters 7, 8, 9, and 10. In each of these sets of chapters you can see how the tests are scored, review the topics likely to be covered on the test, get tips on succeeding at constructed-response tests, take a practice test, and see sample responses and how they were scored.

As you use this book, set the following tasks for yourself:

Become familiar with the test content. Note what the appropriate chapter of the book says about the topics covered in the test you plan to take.

Consider how well you know the content in each subject area. Perhaps you already know that you need to build up your skills in a particular area. If you're not sure, look at the "What to Study" section of the "Preparing for..." chapter, obtain some of the resources that are mentioned there, and skim the topics they cover. If you encounter material that feels unfamiliar or difficult, fold down page corners or insert sticky notes to remind yourself to spend extra time reviewing these topics.

Familiarize yourself with test taking. Chapter 3 explains how constructed-response tests are scored and contains valuable tips on how to succeed on a test in this format. Then you can simulate the experience of the test by taking a practice test within the specified time limit of one hour.

Choose a time and place where you will not be interrupted or distracted. After you complete the test, you can see sample responses that scored well, scored poorly, or scored in-between. By examining these sample responses, you can focus on the aspects of your own practice response that were successful and unsuccessful. This knowledge will help you plan any additional studying you might need.

Register for the test and consider last-minute tips. Consult www.ets.org/praxis/index.html to learn how to register for the test, and review the checklist in chapter 10 to make sure you are ready for the test.

You can accomplish the second and third tasks either on your own or as part of a class or study group.

Using this book to prepare on your own

If you are working by yourself to prepare for a *Science* constructed-response test, you may find it helpful to fill out the Study Plan Sheet in appendix A. This work sheet will help you to focus on what topics you need to study most, identify materials that will help you study, and set a schedule for doing the studying. The last item is particularly important if you know you tend to put off work.

Using this book as part of a study group

People who have a lot of studying to do sometimes find it helpful to form a study group with others who are preparing toward the same goal. Study groups give members opportunities to ask questions and get detailed answers. In a group, some members usually have a better understanding of certain topics, while others in the group may be better at other topics. As members take turns explaining concepts to each other, everyone builds self-confidence. If the group encounters a question that none of the members can answer well, the members can go as a group to a teacher or other expert and get answers efficiently. Because study groups schedule regular meetings, group members study in a more disciplined fashion. They also gain emotional support. The group should be large enough so that various people can contribute various kinds of knowledge, but small enough so that it stays focused. Often, three to six people make a good-sized group.

Here are some ways to use this book as part of a study group:

Plan the group's study program. Parts of the Study Plan Sheet in appendix A can help to structure your group's study program. By filling out the first five columns and sharing the work sheets, everyone will learn more about your group's mix of abilities and about the resources (such as textbooks) that members can share with the group. In the sixth column ("Dates planned for study of content"), you can create an overall schedule for your group's study program.

Plan individual group sessions. At the end of each session, the group should decide what specific topics will be covered at the next meeting and who will present each topic. Use the topic headings and subheadings in the chapter that covers the topics for the test you will take.

Prepare your presentation for the group. When it's your turn to be presenter, prepare something that's more than a lecture. Write five to ten original questions to pose to the group. Practicing writing actual questions can help you better understand the topics covered on the test as well as the types of questions you will encounter on the test. It will also give other members of the group extra practice at answering questions.

Take the practice test together. The idea of the practice test is to simulate an actual administration of the test, so scheduling a test session with the group will add to the realism and will also help boost everyone's confidence.

Learn from the results of the practice test. For each test, use the corresponding chapter with the correct answers to score each other's answer sheets. Then plan one or more study sessions based on the questions that group members got wrong. For example, each group member might be responsible for a question that he or she got wrong and could use it as a model to create an original question to pose to the group, together with an explanation of the correct answer modeled after the explanations in this study guide.

Whether you decide to study alone or with a group, remember that the best way to prepare is to have an organized plan. The plan should set goals based on specific topics and skills that you need to learn, and it should commit you to a realistic set of deadlines for meeting these goals. Then you need to discipline yourself to stick with your plan and accomplish your goals on schedule.

Chapter 2
Background Information on The Praxis Series™ Assessments

► ► ► ► ► ► ► ► ► ► ► ►

What Are The Praxis Series Subject Assessments?

The Praxis Series Subject Assessments are designed by Educational Testing Service (ETS) to assess your knowledge of the subject area you plan to teach, and they are a part of the licensing procedure in many states. This study guide covers an assessment that tests your knowledge of the actual content you hope to be licensed to teach. Your state has adopted The Praxis Series tests because it wants to be certain that you have achieved a specified level of mastery of your subject area before it grants you a license to teach in a classroom.

The Praxis Series tests are part of a national testing program, meaning that the test covered in this study guide is used in more than one state. The advantage of taking Praxis tests is that if you want to move to another state that uses The Praxis Series tests, you can transfer your scores to that state. Passing scores are set by states, however, so if you are planning to apply for licensure in another state, you may find that passing scores are different. You can find passing scores for all states that use The Praxis Series tests in the *Understanding Your Praxis Scores* pamphlet, available either in your college's School of Education or by calling (609) 771-7395.

What Is Licensure?

Licensure in any area—medicine, law, architecture, accounting, cosmetology—is an assurance to the public that the person holding the license has demonstrated a certain level of competence. The phrase used in licensure is that the person holding the license *will do no harm*. In the case of teacher licensing, a license tells the public that the person holding the license can be trusted to educate children competently and professionally.

Because a license makes such a serious claim about its holder, licensure tests are usually quite demanding. In some fields licensure tests have more than one part and last for more than one day. Candidates for licensure in all fields plan intensive study as part of their professional preparation: some join study groups, others study alone. But preparing to take a licensure test is, in all cases, a professional activity. Because it assesses your entire body of knowledge or skill for the field you want to enter, preparing for a licensure exam takes planning, discipline, and sustained effort. Studying thoroughly is highly recommended.

Why Does My State Require The Praxis Series Assessments?

Your state chose The Praxis Series Assessments because the tests assess the breadth and depth of content—called the "domain" of the test—that your state wants its teachers to possess before they begin to teach. The level of content knowledge, reflected in the passing score, is based on recommendations of panels of teachers and teacher educators in each subject area in each state. The state licensing agency and, in some states, the state legislature ratify the passing scores that have been recommended by panels of teachers. You can find out the passing score required for The Praxis Series Assessments in your state by looking in the pamphlet *Understanding Your Praxis Scores*, which is free from ETS (see above). If you look through this pamphlet, you will see that not all states use the same test modules, and even when they do, the passing scores can differ from state to state.

What Kinds of Tests Are The Praxis Series Subject Assessments?

Two kinds of tests comprise The Praxis Series Subject Assessments: multiple choice (for which you select your answer from a list of choices) and constructed response (for which you write a response of your own). Multiple-choice tests can survey a wider domain because they can ask more questions in a limited period of time. Constructed-response tests have far fewer questions, but the questions require you to demonstrate the depth of your knowledge in the area covered.

What Do the Tests Measure?

The Praxis Series Subject Assessments are tests of content knowledge. They measure your understanding of the subject area you want to teach. The multiple-choice tests measure a broad range of knowledge across your content area. The constructed-response tests measure your ability to explain in depth a few essential topics in your subject area. The content-specific pedagogy tests, most of which are constructed-response, measure your understanding of how to teach certain fundamental concepts in your field. The tests do not measure your actual teaching ability, however. They measure your knowledge of your subject and of how to teach it. The teachers in your field who help us design and write these tests, and the states that require these tests, do so in the belief that knowledge of subject area is the first requirement for licensing. Your teaching ability is a skill that is measured in other ways: observation, videotaped teaching, or portfolios are typically used by states to measure teaching ability. Teaching combines many complex skills, only some of which can be measured by a single test. The Praxis Series Subject Assessments are designed to measure how thoroughly you understand the material in the subject areas in which you want to be licensed to teach.

How Were These Tests Developed?

ETS began the development of The Praxis Series Subject Assessments with a survey. For each subject, teachers around the country in various teaching situations were asked to judge which knowledge and skills a beginning teacher in that subject needs to possess. Professors in schools of education who prepare teachers were asked the same questions. These responses were ranked in order of importance and sent out to hundreds of teachers for review. All of the responses to these surveys (called "job analysis surveys") were analyzed to summarize the judgments of these professionals. From their consensus, we developed the specifications for the multiple-choice and constructed-response tests. Each subject area had a committee of practicing teachers and teacher educators who wrote these specifications (guidelines). The specifications were reviewed and eventually approved by teachers. From the test specifications, groups of teachers and professional test developers created test questions.

When your state adopted The Praxis Series Subject Assessments, local panels of practicing teachers and teacher educators in each subject area met to examine the tests question by question and evaluate each question for its relevance to beginning teachers in your state. This is called a "validity study." A test is considered "valid" for a job if it measures what people must know and be able to do on that job. For the test to be adopted in your state, teachers in your state must judge that it is valid.

These teachers and teacher educators also performed a "standard-setting study"; that is, they went through the tests question by question and decided, through a rigorous process, how many questions a beginning teacher should be able to answer correctly. From this study emerged a recommended passing score. The final passing score was approved by your state's Department of Education.

In other words, throughout the development process, practitioners in the teaching field—teachers and teacher educators—have determined what the tests would contain. The practitioners in your state determined which tests would be used for licensure in your subject area and helped decide what score would be needed to achieve licensure. This is how professional licensure works in most fields: those who are already licensed oversee the licensing of new practitioners. When you pass The Praxis Series Subject Assessments, you and the practitioners in your state can be assured that you have the knowledge required to begin practicing your profession.

Chapter 3
Succeeding on the Science Content Essays Tests

▶   ▶   ▶   ▶   ▶   ▶   ▶   ▶   ▶   ▶   ▶   ▶

The goal of this chapter is to help you improve your skills in writing answers to constructed-response questions related to biology, chemistry, physics, or general science. This chapter will provide you with background information, advice from experts, and an opportunity to examine sample questions and responses closely so that you can improve your skills in writing appropriate responses. This chapter also provides information on how your responses on this test will be scored.

What You Should Know about How the Science Content Essays Tests Are Scored

As you build your skills in writing answers to constructed-response questions, it is important to keep in mind the process used to score the tests. If you understand the process by which your test is scored, you may have a better context in which to think about your strategies for success.

How the tests are scored

After each test administration, test books are returned to Educational Testing Service (ETS). The test booklets in which constructed-response answers are written are sent to the location of the scoring session.

The scoring sessions usually take place over two days. The sessions are led by scoring leaders, highly qualified life science and physical science teachers who have many years of experience scoring test questions. All of the remaining scorers are experienced science teachers and teacher educators. An effort is made to balance experienced scorers with newer scorers at each session; the experienced scorers provide continuity with past sessions, and the new scorers ensure that new ideas and perspectives are considered and that the pool of scorers remains large enough to cover the test's needs throughout the year.

Preparing to train the scorers

The scoring leaders meet several days before the scoring session to assemble the materials for the training portion of the main session. Training scorers is a rigorous process, and it is designed to ensure that each response gets a score that is consistent both with the scores given to other papers and with the overall scoring philosophy and criteria established for the test when it was designed.

The scoring leaders first review the General Scoring Guide, which contains the overall criteria, stated in general terms, for awarding the appropriate score. The leaders also review and discuss—and make additions to, if necessary—the Question-Specific Scoring Guide, which serves as an application of the general guide to each specific question on the test. The question-specific guide cannot cover every possible response the scorers will see, but it is designed to give enough examples to guide the scorers in making accurate judgments about the variety of answers they will encounter.

To begin identifying appropriate training materials for an individual question, the scoring leaders first read through many responses to get a sense of the range of answers. They then choose a set of benchmarks, selecting one paper at each score level. These benchmarks serve as solid representative examples of the kind of response that meets the scoring criteria at each score level and are considered the foundation for score standards throughout the session.

The scoring leaders then choose a larger set of test-taker responses to serve as sample papers. These sample papers represent the wide variety of possible responses that the scorers might see. The sample papers serve as the basis for practice scoring at the scoring session, so that the scorers can rehearse how they will apply the scoring criteria before they begin.

The process of choosing a set of benchmark responses and a set of sample responses is followed systematically for each question to be scored at the session. After the scoring leaders are done with their selections and discussions, the sets they have chosen are photocopied and inserted into the scorers' folders in preparation for the session.

Training at the main scoring session

At the scoring session, the scorers are placed into groups according to the question(s) they are assigned to score. New scorers are distributed equally across all groups. One of the scoring leaders is placed with each group. The chief scorer is the person who has overall authority over the scoring session and plays a variety of key roles in training and in ensuring consistent and fair scores.

For each question, the training session proceeds in the same way:

1. All scorers carefully read through the question they will be scoring.
2. All scorers review the General Scoring Guide and the Question-Specific Scoring Guide for the question.
3. The leader guides the scorers through the set of benchmark responses, explaining in detail why each response received the score it did. Scorers are encouraged to ask questions and share their perspectives.
4. Scorers practice on the set of sample responses chosen by the leaders. The leader polls the scorers on what scores they awarded and then leads a discussion to ensure that there is consensus about the scoring criteria and how they are to be applied.
5. One or more sets of non-scored papers are then read by each member of the group, following which the group discusses what scores individual scorers would award according to the scoring criteria. The papers are then scored using a consensus scoring technique.
6. When the leader is confident that the scorers for that question will apply the criteria consistently and accurately, the actual scoring begins.

Quality-control processes

A number of procedures are followed to ensure that accuracy of scoring is maintained during the scoring session. Most importantly, each response is scored twice, with the first scorer's decision hidden from the second scorer. If the two scores for a paper are the same or differ by only one point, the scoring for that paper is considered complete, and the test taker will be awarded the sum of the two scores. If the two scores differ by more than one point, the response is scored by a scoring leader, who has not seen the decisions made by the other two scorers. If this third score is midway between the first two scores, the test taker's score for the question is the sum of the first two scores; otherwise, it is the sum of the third score and whichever of the first two scores is closer to it.

Another way of maintaining scoring accuracy is through back-reading. Throughout the session, the leader for each question checks random samples of scores awarded by all the scorers. If the leader finds that a scorer is not applying the scoring criteria appropriately, that scorer is given more training.

At the beginning of the second day of reading, additional sets of papers are scored using the consensus method described above. This helps ensure that the scorers are refreshed on the scoring criteria and are applying them consistently.

Finally, the scoring session is designed so that several different scorers (usually four) read different parts of any single test taker's responses and contribute separately to the total score. This minimizes the effects of a scorer who might score slightly more rigorously or generously than other scorers.

The entire scoring process—general and specific scoring guides, standardized benchmarks and samples, consensus scoring, adjudication procedures, back-reading, and rotation of test questions to a variety of scorers—is applied consistently and systematically at every scoring session to ensure comparable scores for each administration and across all administrations of the test.

Advice from the experts

Scorers who have scored thousands of real tests offer the following practical pieces of advice.

1. **Read and answer the question accurately.** Be sure to dissect the parts of the question and analyze what each part is asking you to do. If the question asks you to *describe* or *discuss,* keep those requirements in mind when composing your response—do not just give a list.

2. **Answer everything that is being asked in the question.** This seems simple, but many test takers fail to provide a complete response. If a question asks you to do three distinct things in your response, don't give a response to just two of those things. No matter how well you write about those two things, the scorers will not award you full credit.

3. **Give a thorough and detailed response.** Your response must indicate to the scorers that you have a thorough understanding of the applicable science principles and guidelines. The scorers will not read anything into your response that is not expressly written. If something is not written, they do not know that you know it and will not give you credit for it.

4. **Do not change the question or challenge the basis of the question.** Stay focused on the question that is asked. You will receive no credit if you choose to answer another question or indicate that what the question is asking is inappropriate.

General Scoring Guide

The following general guide provides the rubrics for scoring the constructed-response questions on the *Biology, Chemistry, Physics,* or *General Science* tests.

Each question in these tests is scored according to the rubrics in the scoring guide below, on a scale of 0 to 5.

<u>Score</u>	<u>Comment</u>
5	Demonstrates a ***superior*** understanding of the science concepts required by the question • gives clear, accurate, and well-reasoned explanations • uses accurate scientific terminology throughout • when required, provides accurate and well-chosen supporting evidence (e.g., physical laws, data, definitions, examples) • any diagrams, tables, and graphs presented are complete, clear, accurate, and well organized
4	Demonstrates a ***strong*** understanding of the science concepts required by the question • gives clear, accurate, and logical explanations • uses accurate scientific terminology • when required, provides accurate and relevant supporting evidence (e.g., physical laws, data, definitions. examples) • any diagrams, tables, and graphs presented are generally complete, accurate, and organized

3   Demonstrates an *adequate* understanding of the science concepts required by most parts of the question
- gives generally clear, accurate, and logical explanations
- uses some accurate scientific terminology
- when required, provides generally accurate and relevant supporting evidence (e.g., physical laws, data, definitions, examples)
- any diagrams, tables, and graphs presented are sufficiently complete and accurate

2   Demonstrates a *limited* understanding of the science concepts required by the question, as evidenced by <u>one or more</u> of the following characteristics:
- may give insufficiently accurate and/or poorly developed explanations
- may lack accurate scientific terminology
- when required, may give very limited supporting evidence (e.g., physical laws, data, definitions, examples)
- any diagrams, tables, and graphs presented may be incomplete and/or inaccurate

1   Demonstrates *very little* understanding of the science concepts required by the question, as evidenced by <u>one or more</u> of the following characteristics:
- may give inaccurate, illogical, incoherent, or seriously incomplete explanations
- may fail to use accurate scientific terminology
- may give little or no supporting evidence (e.g., physical laws, data, definitions, examples)
- any diagrams, tables, and graphs presented may be seriously inaccurate, confusing, or incomplete

0   Completely inaccurate or inappropriate, blank, or off topic.

Question-Specific Scoring Guides

After a question is developed, three or four knowledgeable experts develop ideas for model answers. These model answers are used to develop a Question-Specific Scoring Guide that creates a list of specific examples of responses that would receive various scores. This list contains examples of various answers, not *all* possible answers. The Question-Specific Scoring Guide, which is based on model answers, provides the basis for choosing the papers that serve as the benchmarks and sample papers used for training the scorers at the scoring session. During the scoring sessions, specific examples can be added to the scoring guide, and papers can be added as samples for future readings.

Given the information above about how constructed-responses are scored and what the scorers are looking for in successful responses, you are now ready to look at specific questions, suggestions of how to approach the questions, and sample responses and scores given to those responses.

Chapter 4
Preparing for the Science Content Essays Tests

▶ ▶ ▶ ▶ ▶ ▶ ▶ ▶ ▶ ▶ ▶ ▶

The goal of this chapter is to provide you with strategies for reading, analyzing, and understanding the questions on the *Biology, Chemistry, Physics,* and *General Science: Content Essays* tests and for outlining and writing successful responses.

Introduction to the Tests

The *Biology, Chemistry, Physics,* or *General Science: Content Essays* tests are intended to assess the knowledge and competencies considered necessary for a prospective teacher of biology, chemistry, physics, or general science in a secondary school. Each one-hour test consists of three equally weighted constructed-response questions. One question is designed to test knowledge of scientific principles and concepts. A second question is designed to evaluate understanding of the basic scientific methodology and ability to design and carry out a valid scientific experiment. A third question is designed to assess understanding of the impact scientific applications may have on society.

The *Biology: Content Essays* test is designed to measure the subject-area knowledge and competencies considered necessary for a beginning teacher of biology in a secondary school. The test assesses test takers' ability to use and analyze important biological concepts. The three questions focus on biology content that includes knowledge of cell and molecular biology, genetics and evolution, and organismal biology and ecology. Two questions test both an area of content knowledge and a specific scientific skill; the third question covers science, technology, and society.

The *Chemistry: Content Essays* test is designed to measure the knowledge and competencies considered necessary for a beginning teacher of chemistry in a secondary school. The test assesses test takers' ability to use and analyze critical science concepts and to integrate knowledge from science, technology, and society. The three questions focus on chemistry content that includes knowledge of structure/property correlations, chemical reactions, and the impact of chemistry on technology and society. Two questions test both an area of content knowledge and a specific scientific skill; the third question covers science, technology, and society.

The *Physics: Content Essays* test is designed to measure the knowledge and competencies considered necessary for a beginning teacher of physics in a secondary school. The test assesses test takers' ability to use and analyze critical science concepts and to integrate knowledge from science, technology, and society. The questions focus on physics content that includes knowledge of matter and energy, fields and waves, and the impact of physics on technology and society. Two questions test both an area of content knowledge and a specific scientific skill; the third question covers science, technology, and society.

The *General Science: Content Essays* test is designed to measure the knowledge and competencies considered necessary for a beginning teacher of general science in a secondary school. The questions focus on one of the content areas of physical science, life science, or earth and space science. Each question is framed within a specific scientific skill or context: concepts, models, systems, and patterns; data analysis, experimental design, and investigations; or science, technology, and society. Thus, for example, a question might involve the content area of life science and be framed within the perspective of models or systems or how that issue is related to problems in science, technology, and society.

What to Study

Success on this test is not simply a matter of learning more about how to respond to constructed-response questions. Success on the test also requires real knowledge of the field.

It therefore would serve you well to read books and review notes in the areas of basic scientific principles and concepts, plus experiment design and data collection, and to have some awareness of the impact of technology on society, including the general subject of bioethics. There are many good review books on these topics available in your local library or bookstores.

For information on societal impact, it is recommended that you have a general knowledge of current events in science and technology. Information on bioethics can be found at Web sites such as the National Institute of Health "Bioethics Resources on the Web" page at www.nih.gov/sigs/bioethics or *The American Journal of Bioethics* Web site at www.bioethics.net.

You may consult with Web sites of some subject-specific professional organizations, for example, The American Institute of Biological Sciences (www.aibs.org), American Chemical Society (www.acs.org), American Physical Society (www.aps.org), American Geological Institute (www.agiweb.org), and National Science Teachers Association (www.nsta.org).

Note: The test is not based on these resources, and they do not necessarily cover every topic that may be included on the test.

Understanding What the Questions Are Asking

It is impossible to write a successful response to a question unless you thoroughly understand the question. Often test takers jump into their written response without taking enough time to analyze exactly what the question is asking, how many different parts of the question need to be addressed, and how the information in the accompanying charts or tables needs to be addressed. The time you invest in making sure you understand what the question is asking will very likely pay off in better performance, as long as you budget your time and do not spend a large proportion of the available time just reading the question.

Sample Question 1

To illustrate the importance of understanding the question before you begin writing, let's start with a sample question:

The appearance of the Moon as observed from a given location on Earth changes each day as a result of the relative positions and motions of Earth, the Moon, and the Sun. The observed changes during one lunar month are known as the phases of the Moon.

Diagram and explain how the phases of the Moon are produced by these relative motions.

Key components of the question

- There are two parts to the question—the diagram and the explanation.
- A clearly labeled, accurate, and complete diagram is needed.
- An indication of the scale of the diagram is needed.
- A written explanation must clearly explain the relative movements of Earth, the Sun, and the Moon that result in the phases of the Moon.

Organizing your response

Successful responses start with successful planning, either with an outline or with another form of notes. By planning your response, you greatly decrease the chances that you will forget to answer any part of the question. You increase the chances of creating a well-organized response, which is something the scorers look for. Your note-taking space also gives you a place in which to jot down thoughts whenever you think of them—for example, when you have an idea about one part of the question while you are writing your response to another part. Like taking time to make sure you understand what the question is asking, planning your response is time well invested, although you must budget your time so that you leave sufficient time to write your response.

To illustrate a possible strategy for planning a response, let us focus again on the sample question introduced in the previous section. We analyzed the question and found that it necessitated a two-part response: a diagram and an explanation. You might begin by jotting down those parts on your notes page, leaving space under each. This will ensure that you address each part when you begin writing.

Sample notes—main parts to be answered

> I. Diagram explaining the relative positions/motions of Earth, the Moon, and the Sun
>
> II. Explanation of diagram/phases of the Moon

You then might quickly fill out the main ideas you want to address in each part, like this:

Sample notes—ideas under each main part

> I. Diagram explaining the relative positions/motions of Earth, the Moon, and the Sun
>
> > a. the Moon rotates around Earth (close)
> >
> > b. Earth rotates around the Sun (far)
>
> II. Explanation of diagram/phases of the Moon
>
> > a. Moonshine is light from the Sun reflected off of the Moon
> >
> > b. the Moon orbits Earth in just over 28 days
> >
> > c. Earth orbits the Sun in just over 365 days
> >
> > d. the part of the Moon illuminated by the Sun always faces the Sun
> >
> > e. The part of the Moon that is illuminated changes as the Moon orbits Earth
> >
> > f. occasionally the Moon blocks the Sun or Earth blocks the light hitting the Moon (eclipses)

These are key characteristics that the scorers will look for:
- Answer all parts of the question.
- Give reasons for your answers.
- Demonstrate subject-specific knowledge in your answer.

Now look at your notes and add any ideas that would address these characteristics. Notice below the additions that are made.

Sample notes, with added ideas

I. Diagram explaining the relative positions/motions of Earth, the Moon, and the Sun

    a. the Moon rotates around Earth (close)

    b. Earth rotates around the Sun (far)

Phases of Moon are New, First Quarter, Full, and Third Quarter. As Moon gets brighter it is waxing, dimmer it is waning.
Make sure in diagram that Moon is closer to Earth than to Sun, and Moon is smaller than Earth, which is smaller than Sun
Note that objects are not to scale (Sun is 93M miles away, Moon is 0.25M miles away)

II. Explanation of diagram/phases of the Moon

    a. Moonshine is light from the Sun reflected off of the Moon

Moon doesn't give off light of its own

    b. the Moon orbits Earth in just over 28 days

    c. Earth orbits the Sun in just over 365 days

All orbits are close to being in the same plane. The plane of the Moon's orbit is 5 degrees out of Earth's orbit—that is why we don't get eclipses every month.

    d. the part of the Moon illuminated by the Sun always faces the Sun

    e. The part of the Moon that is illuminated changes as the Moon orbits Earth

The Moon keeps its same face toward us (period of rotation = period of orbit)

    f. Occasionally the Moon blocks the Sun or Earth blocks the light hitting the Moon (eclipses)

Mention eclipses only if time

You have now created the skeleton of your written response.

Writing your response

Now the important step of writing your response begins. The scorers will not consider your notes when they score your paper, so it is crucial that you integrate all the important ideas from your notes into your actual written response.

Some test takers believe that every written response on a Praxis™ test has to be in formal essay form: First, with an introductory paragraph, then paragraphs with the response to the question, and finally, a concluding paragraph. This is the case for very few Praxis tests (e.g., *English* and *Writing*). The *Biology*, *Chemistry*, *Physics*, and *General Science: Content Essays* tests do **not** require formal essays, so you should use techniques that allow you to communicate information efficiently and clearly. For example, you can use bulleted or numbered lists, or a diagram, or a combination of essay and diagram.

Returning to our sample question, note in the sample response below how the outline of the response to the question can be transformed into the final written response (this is an actual response by a test taker).

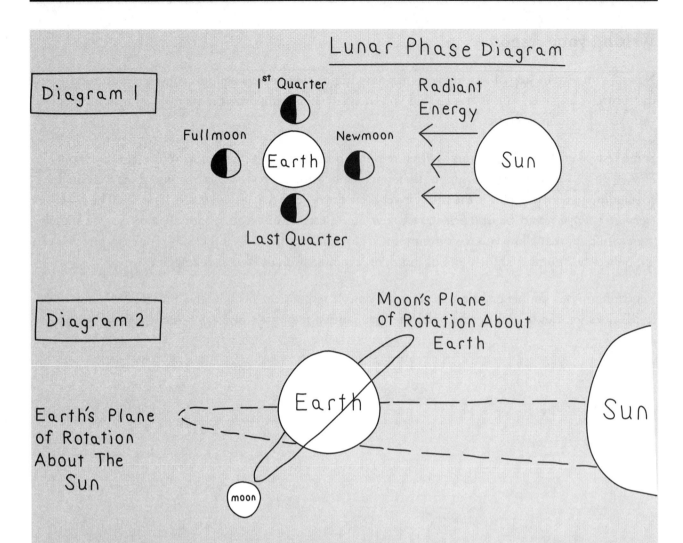

Lunar Phase Diagram

Diagram 1

1st Quarter

Fullmoon   Newmoon

Earth

Last Quarter

Radiant Energy

Sun

Diagram 2

Moon's Plane of Rotation About Earth

Earth's Plane of Rotation About The Sun

Earth

moon

Sun

The Lunar phases are produced by the relative motions and positions of the Earth, Moon, and Sun. The lunar phases progress as the moon orbits the Earth and the illuminated portions of the moon change from a position on the Earth.

Beginning with the new moon as shown on diagram 1, the portion of the moon that is illuminated by the sun is hidden from view on earth. As the phase continues with the following nights, the moon progresses in its orbit of the Earth enough to allow increasing amounts of the illuminated portion of the moon to be seen on the Earth until the 1st Quarter is seen approximately seven days after the new moon was observed. The lunar phase continues until a Full moon is observed as the maximum amount of illuminated moon can be seen on earth. The amount of illuminated moon then decreases through 2nd quarter until the new moon is reached at the end of the monthly lunar phase.

Lunar eclipses occur when the lunar orbit becomes parallel with the Earth's plane of orbit around the sun. Lunar eclipses are observed because the moon is shielded from the suns light by the earth. Solar eclipses occur similarly, but the moon would block the suns light from position on the Earth.

The change in the lunar rise and set is due to the lunar axis of rotation about the Earth and also the Earth's orbit about the Sun. As diagram 2 illustrates, the lunar orbit is not always parallel with the Earth's plane of rotation about the Sun.

Sample Question 2

Now let's look at another sample question:

Discuss the Hardy-Weinberg principle. In your discussion, include the major assumptions that must be met in order for a population to remain in Hardy-Weinberg equilibrium.

Key components of the question

There are two major components to the question:

- A general discussion of the principle

- A list and discussion of the major assumptions that must be met for a population to remain in Hardy-Weinberg equilibrium.

Sample notes—main parts to be answered

> I. Description of Hardy-Weinberg principle
> II. List and discuss major assumptions

You then might quickly fill out the main ideas you want to address in each part, like this:

Sample notes—ideas under each main part

> I. Description of Hardy-Weinberg principle
>   What is the Hardy-Weinberg principle?
>   What does it do?
>   How does it work?

> II. List and discuss major assumptions
>   5 major assumptions for equilibrium to occur

Now look at your notes and add any details that would address these characteristics. Notice below the additions that are made.

Sample notes, with added ideas

> I. Description of Hardy-Weinberg principle
>   What is the Hardy-Weinberg principle?
>
> - Tool for measuring effect of selective forces on a breeding population
>
> What does it do?
>
> - Describes mathematical relationship between frequency of alleles and genotypes in a population.
>
> How does it work?
>
> - Formula is $p^2 + 2pq + q^2 = 1$
>   - ✓ p = frequency of dominant allele
>   - ✓ q = frequency of recessive allele
> - By knowing the percentage of the recessive genotype in a population, one can determine the allelic frequencies.
> - Frequencies of alleles in gene pool will remain constant (H-W equilibrium) only if all assumptions of the model are met.
>
> II. Assumptions
> - Population very large
> - Mating within population completely random
> - No mutations occur
> - No gene flow into or out of population
> - All genotypes have equal chance of reproductive success

You have now created the skeleton of your written response. Returning to our sample question, note in the sample response below how the outline done earlier in the chapter can be transformed into the final written response (this is an actual response by a test taker).

The Hardy-Weinberg principle talks about a population—that is in a genetic equilibrium if p is the frequency of the dominant allele of the given gene and q is the recessive allele of that gene than $p+q=1.00$ and also $p^2+2pq+q^2=1.0000$ (or 1). Where p^2 represents the frequency of homozygous dominant genotypes, $2pq$ represents the heterozygous dominant genotypes and q^2 represents the homozygous recessive genotypes.

There are five criteria that must be met for a population to remain in the Hardy-Weinberg equilibrium.

1. The populations must be large. This is because of the error that is inherent with a small sample size. If the population is large, there is a more accurate representation of the frequency of a given allele.

2. The population must be panmictic. In other words, random mating must occur if there is not random mating, this will alter the frequencies of genotypes passed on to the next generation, each generation.

3. There must be no mutation. Mutation will change the genotype, thus changing the frequencies and equilibrium will not be met.

4. There must be no migration. This would prevent genotypes from leaving and/or new genotypes from entering, both which would alter the frequencies of the alleles.

5. There must be no selection. Selection favors certain phenotypes which are caused by their respective genotype. If on genotype is selected for or against, the frequencies of alleles will be changed.

A population with these five characteristics is in Hardy-Weinberg equilibrium. To determine the frequency of an allele or of a genotype the equations and can be used. If one of the five characteristics is missing, the population will no longer be in equilibrium.

Chapter 5
Practice Questions—Science Content Essays Tests

▶   ▶   ▶   ▶   ▶   ▶   ▶   ▶   ▶   ▶   ▶   ▶

Now that you have worked through strategies and preparation for the Science Content Essays tests, you should answer the following practice questions. These questions are actual test questions, now retired. You will probably find it helpful to simulate actual testing conditions, giving yourself 20 minutes to work on each of the questions. You can use the lined answer pages provided if you wish.

Keep in mind that the test you take at an actual administration will have different questions. You should not expect your level of performance to be exactly the same as when you take the test at an actual administration, since numerous factors affect a person's performance in any given testing situation.

When you have finished the practice questions, you can read through the sample responses with scorer annotations in chapter 6.

THE PRAXIS SERIES

Professional Assessments for Beginning Teachers®

Educational Testing Service

TEST NAME:

Biology: Content Essays (0233)
Chemistry: Content Essays (0242)
Physics: Content Essays (0262)
General Science: Content Essays (0433)

Time—80 Minutes

4 Questions

NO CALCULATORS PERMITTED

PERIODIC TABLE OF THE ELEMENTS

DO NOT DETACH FROM BOOK.

1	2	3	4	5	6	7	8	9	10	11	12	13	14	15	16	17	18
1 **H** 1.0079																	2 **He** 4.0026
3 **Li** 6.941	4 **Be** 9.012											5 **B** 10.811	6 **C** 12.011	7 **N** 14.007	8 **O** 16.00	9 **F** 19.00	10 **Ne** 20.179
11 **Na** 22.99	12 **Mg** 24.30											13 **Al** 26.98	14 **Si** 28.09	15 **P** 30.974	16 **S** 32.06	17 **Cl** 35.453	18 **Ar** 39.948
19 **K** 39.10	20 **Ca** 40.08	21 **Sc** 44.96	22 **Ti** 47.90	23 **V** 50.94	24 **Cr** 52.00	25 **Mn** 54.938	26 **Fe** 55.85	27 **Co** 58.93	28 **Ni** 58.69	29 **Cu** 63.55	30 **Zn** 65.39	31 **Ga** 69.72	32 **Ge** 72.59	33 **As** 74.92	34 **Se** 78.96	35 **Br** 79.90	36 **Kr** 83.80
37 **Rb** 85.47	38 **Sr** 87.62	39 **Y** 88.91	40 **Zr** 91.22	41 **Nb** 92.91	42 **Mo** 95.94	43 **Tc** (98)	44 **Ru** 101.1	45 **Rh** 102.91	46 **Pd** 106.42	47 **Ag** 107.87	48 **Cd** 112.41	49 **In** 114.82	50 **Sn** 118.71	51 **Sb** 121.75	52 **Te** 127.60	53 **I** 126.91	54 **Xe** 131.29
55 **Cs** 132.91	56 **Ba** 137.33	57 ***La** 138.91	72 **Hf** 178.49	73 **Ta** 180.95	74 **W** 183.85	75 **Re** 186.21	76 **Os** 190.2	77 **Ir** 192.2	78 **Pt** 195.08	79 **Au** 196.97	80 **Hg** 200.59	81 **Tl** 204.38	82 **Pb** 207.2	83 **Bi** 208.98	84 **Po** (209)	85 **At** (210)	86 **Rn** (222)
87 **Fr** (223)	88 **Ra** 226.02	89 **†Ac** 227.03	104 **Rf** (261)	105 **Db** (262)	106 **Sg** (263)	107 **Bh** (262)	108 **Hs** (265)	109 **Mt** (266)	110 **§** (269)	111 **§** (272)	112 **§** (277)						

*Lanthanide Series

58 **Ce** 140.12	59 **Pr** 140.91	60 **Nd** 144.24	61 **Pm** (145)	62 **Sm** 150.4	63 **Eu** 151.97	64 **Gd** 157.25	65 **Tb** 158.93	66 **Dy** 162.50	67 **Ho** 164.93	68 **Er** 167.26	69 **Tm** 168.93	70 **Yb** 173.04	71 **Lu** 174.97

†Actinide Series

90 **Th** 232.04	91 **Pa** 231.04	92 **U** 238.03	93 **Np** 237.05	94 **Pu** (244)	95 **Am** (243)	96 **Cm** (247)	97 **Bk** (247)	98 **Cf** (251)	99 **Es** (252)	100 **Fm** (257)	101 **Md** (258)	102 **No** (259)	103 **Lr** (260)

§Not yet named

TABLE OF INFORMATION

Electron rest mass	$m_e = 9.11 \times 10^{-31}$ kilogram
Proton rest mass	$m_p = 1.672 \times 10^{-27}$ kilogram
Neutron rest mass	$m_n = 1.675 \times 10^{-27}$ kilogram
Magnitude of the electron charge	$e = 1.60 \times 10^{-19}$ coulomb
Bohr radius	$a_0 = 5.29 \times 10^{-11}$ meter
Avogadro number	$N_A = 6.02 \times 10^{23}$ per mole
Universal gas constant	$R = 8.314$ joules /(mole $\cdot$ K)
	$= 0.0821$ L $\cdot$ atm /(mole $\cdot$ K)
Boltzmann constant	$k = 1.38 \times 10^{-23}$ joule/K
Planck constant	$h = 6.63 \times 10^{-34}$ joule $\cdot$ second
	$= 4.14 \times 10^{-15}$ eV $\cdot$ second
Speed of light	$c = 3.00 \times 10^{8}$ meters/second
Vacuum permittivity	$\epsilon_0 = 8.85 \times 10^{-12}$ coulomb^2/(newton $\cdot$ meter^2)
Vacuum permeability	$\mu_0 = 4\pi \times 10^{-7}$ newton /ampere^2
Coulomb constant	$\frac{1}{4}\pi \epsilon_0 = 8.99 \times 10^{9}$ newtons $\cdot$ meter^2/coulomb^2
Universal gravitational constant	$G = 6.67 \times 10^{-11}$ newton $\cdot$ meter^2/kilogram^2
Acceleration due to gravity	$g = 9.8$ meters/ second^2
1 atmosphere pressure	1 atm $= 1.0 \times 10^{5}$ newtons/meter^2
	$= 1.0 \times 10^{5}$ pascals (Pa)
Faraday constant	$\mathscr{F} = 9.65 \times 10^{4}$ coulombs/mole
1 atomic mass unit	1 amu $= 1.66 \times 10^{-27}$ kilogram
1 electron volt	1 eV $= 1.602 \times 10^{-19}$ joule

For H_2O:

heat of fusion	3.33×10^{2} joules/gram
heat of vaporization	2.26×10^{3} joules/gram
mean specific heat (liquid)	4.19 joules/(gram $\cdot$ K)

Volume of 1 mole of ideal gas at 0°C, 1 atmosphere	22.4 liters

SCIENCE: CONTENT ESSAYS

Question 1

Colorless substrate $\xrightarrow{\text{Enzyme } X}$ Colored product (maximum absorbance at 450 nanometers)

Design an experiment to determine the effects of pH on the activity of enzyme X, which catalyzes the reaction represented above.

- What hypothesis will you test?
- How will you set up your experiment?
- What type of data will you collect and why?
- How would you present and interpret your data?

NOTES

Question 2

Dialysis and kidney transplantation are two medical advances that have made possible the treatment of diseases that were previously untreatable.

(a) List three causes of kidney failure that may necessitate the use of these procedures.

(b) Briefly describe what is involved in the processes of dialysis and kidney transplantation.

(c) Discuss the societal issues that may accompany the use of each of these procedures.

NOTES

Question 3

A region of fixed latitude on a fictional Earthlike planet has the altitude profile shown in the diagram below.

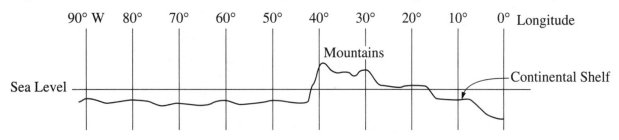

The average value of the acceleration due to gravity on the planet is 5.00 meters per second squared. Over the region depicted in the diagram, the measured values of the acceleration due to gravity are as charted below.

Longitude (°W)	Gravitational Acceleration (m/s²)
0	5.05
10	5.02
20	4.92
30	4.85
40	4.83
50	5.03
60	5.04
70	5.04
80	5.02
90	5.03

Use the information provided in responding to the following.

(a) What geographic feature corresponds to low values of the acceleration due to gravity? Explain how these factors might be correlated.

(b) Local variations in gravitational acceleration in a region are strongly affected by the density of the rock that underlies it. Assume that there are two main types of rock, X and Y, that make up the planet's bedrock. X is more dense than Y. Referring to the profile above, describe which regions of bedrock are most likely to be made of X and Y, respectively. Explain your reasoning in making these assignments.

(c) For surface locations, at about what longitude would water boil at the lowest temperature? What is the reason for this? (Assume that this planet has an atmosphere.)

NOTES

Question 4

The table below summarizes the results of various measurements of the freezing points of a series of samples. Three determinations of freezing point were made for each sample.

Solute Concentration (grams per 100 grams of solvent)	Freezing Point (°C) Trial Number		
	1	2	3
0.0 (pure solvent)	4.6	5.2	4.9
1.0	3.8	3.4	3.6
2.0	2.3	2.7	2.8
4.0	0.6	0.3	2.0

(a) Prepare an appropriate graphical representation of the data.

(b) Do you observe any large discrepancies in the data? If so, where might they come from and how do you interpret them?

(c) Apart from any large discrepancies that might exist, do you observe any small discrepancies in the data? If so, where might they come from and how do you interpret them?

(d) What mathematical relationship between solute concentration and freezing point can be supported by these data? What, if any, additional data would you suggest collecting to support your interpretation of the relationship?

NOTES

Begin your response to Question 1 here.

(Question 1—*Continued*)

(Question 1—*Continued*)

_____

_____

_____

_____

_____

_____

_____

_____

_____

_____

_____

_____

_____

_____

_____

_____

_____

_____

_____

_____

_____

_____

(Question 1—*Continued*)

Begin your response to Question 2 here.

_____

_____

_____

_____

_____

_____

_____

_____

_____

_____

_____

_____

_____

_____

_____

_____

_____

_____

_____

(Question 2—*Continued*)

_____

_____

_____

_____

_____

_____

_____

_____

_____

_____

_____

_____

_____

_____

_____

_____

_____

_____

_____

(Question 2—*Continued*)

(Question 2—*Continued*)

Begin your response to Question 3 here.

(Question 3—*Continued*)

(Question 3—*Continued*)

_____

_____

_____

_____

_____

_____

_____

_____

_____

_____

_____

_____

_____

_____

_____

_____

_____

_____

_____

_____

_____

_____

_____

_____

(Question 3—*Continued*)

Begin your response to Question 4 here.

(Question 4—*Continued*)

(Question 4—*Continued*)

_____

_____

_____

_____

_____

_____

_____

_____

_____

_____

_____

_____

_____

_____

_____

_____

_____

_____

(Question 4—*Continued*)

_____

_____

_____

_____

_____

_____

_____

_____

_____

_____

_____

_____

_____

_____

_____

_____

_____

_____

_____

_____

Chapter 6

Sample Responses and How They Were Scored—
Science Content Essays Tests

▶ ▶ ▶ ▶ ▶ ▶ ▶ ▶ ▶ ▶ ▶ ▶

This chapter presents the General Scoring Guide used to score responses, four practice questions, actual sample responses to each question, and explanations for the scores they received. As discussed in chapter 3, each question on the *Biology, Chemistry, Physics,* or *General Science: Content Essays* tests is scored on a scale from 0 to 5.

General Scoring Guide

<u>Score</u>	<u>Comment</u>
5	Demonstrates a ***superior*** understanding of the science concepts required by the question:

- gives clear, accurate, and well-reasoned explanations

- uses accurate scientific terminology throughout

- when required, provides accurate and well-chosen supporting evidence (e.g., physical laws, data, definitions, examples)

- any diagrams, tables, and graphs presented are complete, clear, accurate, and well organized

4	Demonstrates a ***strong*** understanding of the science concepts required by the question:

- gives clear, accurate, and logical explanations

- uses accurate scientific terminology

- when required, provides accurate and relevant supporting evidence (e.g., physical laws, data, definitions, examples)

- any diagrams, tables, and graphs presented are generally complete, clear, accurate, and organized

3	Demonstrates an ***adequate*** understanding of the science concepts required by most parts of the question:

- gives generally clear, accurate, and logical explanations

- uses some accurate scientific terminology

- when required, provides generally accurate and relevant supporting evidence (e.g., physical laws, data, definitions, examples)

- any diagrams, tables, and graphs presented are sufficiently complete, clear, accurate, and well-organized

2   Demonstrates a *limited* understanding of the science concepts required by the question, as evidenced by <u>one or more</u> of the following characteristics:

- may give insufficiently accurate and/or poorly developed explanations

- may lack accurate scientific terminology

- when required, may give very limited supporting evidence (e.g., physical laws, data, definitions, examples)

- any diagrams, tables, and graphs may be incomplete and/or inaccurate

1   Demonstrates *very little* understanding of the science concepts required by the question, as evidenced by <u>one or more</u> of the following characteristics:

- may give inaccurate, illogical, incoherent, or seriously incomplete explanations

- may fail to use accurate scientific terminology

- may give little or no supporting evidence (e.g., physical laws, data, definitions, examples)

- any diagrams, tables, and graphs may be seriously inaccurate, confusing, or incomplete

0   Completely inaccurate or inappropriate, blank, or off topic

Sample Responses

Following are the four sample questions, with their sample responses. Each response will include the score given and an explanation of the score.

Question 1

Colorless substrate $\xrightarrow{\text{Enzyme } X}$ Colored product (maximum absorbance at 450 nanometers)

Design an experiment to determine the effects of pH on the activity of enzyme *X*, which catalyzes the reaction represented above.

- What hypothesis will you test?

- How will you set up your experiment?

- What type of data will you collect and why?

- How would you present and interpret your data?

We will now look at four actual responses to Question 1 and see how the General Scoring Guide was used to rate each response.

Question 1—Sample Response 1: total score of 4 (out of 5)

The hypothesis to be tested is to determine the effect of pH changes (in the substrate solution) an enzyme X activity

To determine the effect of enzyme X we can look at several factors:
1. color change in the substrate
2. rate of color change
3. depth of color change
4. temperature change

We can look at temperature change to observe changes in heat energy. However, the major effect (as stated by the question) is change in color so we may want to focus initial data collection on items 1, 2, and 3.

To set up the experiment, we need to do serial dilutions of acid in standard samples of the substrate. We also need to do serial dilutions of base in standard sample of the substrate. Obviously we also need a control set of substrate samples.

For example, we add 1 drop of enzyme to a test tube containing 5 drops of substrate and using a stop watch, and white paper background, we note the color change, the time necessary for the color change, and the quality or depth of color change. We can use a spectrophotometer to measure light absorbance of the enzyme-substrate complex to also determine depth of color change This is our control tube.

With a series of tubes we can repeat this process but before we add the enzyme X to the substrate we put in each tube serial dilutions of acid (i.e., .01M, .1M, 1.0M, 2.0M hydrochloric acid). For each tube, note color change, timing of color change and the depth of color change. Each tub also needs to have its pH determined, using pH paper, before and after enzyme X is added.

With another set of test tubes, this experimental process needs to be repeated using serial dilutions of base (i.e. .01 M, .1 M, 1M, 2M sodium hydroxide). Again measure pH with pH paper before and after adding enzyme X. After adding enzyme X, record color change, timing of color change and depth of color change.

Because enzymes are proteins which usually work best in the body's nearly-neutral, slightly acidic milieu, we may expect the lowest and highest pH level (i.e. strongest acidity and basicness) to denature the enzyme X and impede or prevent its catalytic activity on the substrate. To show this, our data table needs to reflect the data collected, but then line graphs can show the relationship between pH and enzyme X activity. Similar graphs can be done for the light absorbance and timing of enzyme X.

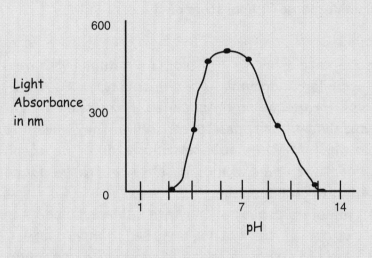

Commentary on Sample Response 1

Strengths:

- Overall answer is strong

- Generally complete

- Includes *most* basic parts of an experiment
  - description of experiment
  - data collection
  - data presentation
  - interpretation of data

- Answers all parts of the question

- Uses good terminology

Weaknesses:

- Hypothesis is not well stated

- Variables are implied, but not described outright

- Replication not discussed

- Didn't use the "450 nm" data given in the prompt. Perhaps does not understand the significance of the measurement.

Question 1—Sample Response 2: total score of 3 (out of 5)

Colorless substrate $\xrightarrow{\text{Enzyme X}}$ Colored product (450 nm max)

In living organisms, enzymes are the catalysts that lower the energy barrier between products and reactants. Thus, they are known as "biological catalysts." Enzymes are proteins. They have a tertiary structure to which only one substrate may bind. The specificity of the arrangement between an enzyme and its substrate suggest the analogy of a "Lock and Key" mechanism.

Since enzymes are proteins, they are subject to the same thermal and acidity restrictions as their other, diverse, counterparts. Changes in pH change the tertiary structure of an enzyme, and consequently alter its specificity for a substrate.

To show that pH does in fact change the conformity of an enzyme, it becomes necessary to conduct an experiment in which differences in pH is the only variable (in other words, all other conditions such as substrate and temperature will remain the same).

Three groups are necessary to conduct the experiment scientifically. The first group will maintain the body's normal pH levels. The other two will have pH lower or higher than the control group.

Data that will be collected will be changes in the amount of product generated; the color of the product, as well as the wavelength absorbance. This will be done for each of the 3 groups.

By conduct the experiment in this fashion, the researcher is guaranteed to obtain results that show changes in the substrate due to changes in pH ALONE. The data will be graphically plotted to show that changes in pH have an adverse effect on the amount and quantity of products generated

Commentary on Sample Response 2

Strengths:

- Most parts of an experiment are present
- Some scientific terminology used

Weaknesses:

- A more *general* answer than sample 1, above
- Replicates implied, but not specifically discussed
- Needs to be more specific about pH levels used
- Should describe *how* absorbance will be measured; eyeball, spectrophotometer, etc.
- Data presentation is weak
- No real discussion of data interpretation

Question 1—Sample Response 3: total score of 2 (out of 5)

We are given a reaction which we know occurs

$$colorless\ substrate \xrightarrow{\ X\ } colored\ product$$

and asked to determine the effects of pH on the activity of enzyme X is the reaction.

The first step is to introduce the idea of the null hypothesis where we will suggest in a formal statement that we believe pH will have no effect on the activity of X in the reaction. This null hypothesis can now be tested experimentally.

We should test for activity of X in various conditions: acidic, neutral, basic and in an altered substrate to serve as a control for comparison. We'll set up four beakers of solutions and prepare the first three to be acidic, neutral or basic by additions of acid or base and testing w/ litmus paper until appropriate. Next we will add enzyme X to each of the four beakers and record the results. The record should include color changes, the time it begins and appears to end, as well as color observed. We could also record temperature change.

The results would be presented for each beaker as a function of time. We could compose graphs of the beakers versus time to completion of reactions as well as graphs which follow temperature changes over time. Comparing the three experimental beakers to the original solution will show whether pH levels are correlated with changes in reactivity of enzyme X. Then we can conclude whether our original hypothesis was correct or not.

Commentary on Sample Response 3

Weaknesses:

- Little scientific terminology
- Very general description of experiment
  - What pH's were used?
  - What is "altered substrate"?
  - How will color change be measured?
  - Data presentation is not clear...no sample graphs
  - Specific pH cannot be measured with litmus paper...need pH paper
  - No mention of replication

Question 1—Sample Response 4: total score of 1 (out of 5)

> Find the activity of enzyme X in the experiment. Set up an experiment on test the effects of pH on the enzyme. We'll use a colorimeter and various type of acids and bases to give us a spectrum. Use of data will be in which the perspective changes from increasing to an abrupt decrease when graphed.
>
> When we draw the graph from the data, we can determine whether or not the activity level of the enzyme is about 450 nm. This will allow us to speculate where the catalysis is.

Commentary on Sample Response 4

Weaknesses:

- Mostly a restate of the prompt
- No real description of an experiment
- Does not answer the question

Question 2

Dialysis and kidney transplantation are two medical advances that have made possible the treatment of diseases that were previously untreatable.

(a) List three causes of kidney failure that may necessitate the use of these procedures.

(b) Briefly describe what is involved in the processes of dialysis and kidney transplantation.

(c) Discuss the societal issues that may accompany the use of each of these procedures.

We will now look at four actual responses to Question 2 and see how the General Scoring Guide was used to rate each response.

Question 2—Sample Response 1: total score of 4/5 (out of 5)
(One reader scored it as 4, the other as 5.)

> The proper functioning of the kidneys are necessary for the maintenance of life. The kidneys help to maintain water and chemical equilibrium in the body.
>
> Kidney failure may result from many causes which include but are not limited to dehydration, hypertension, traumatic injury, and diabetes.
>
> In dialysis a shunt is surgically placed in a person's arm. One part of the shunt is located in a vein and the other part in an artery. During the dialysis procedure a needle connects the shunt to a dialysis machine. Blood leaves the artery and travels through tubing immersed in solution. It is returned to the vein. As it moves through the tubing waste products are removed through diffusion and osmosis. The cleansing solution will have much lower levels of the chemicals which comprise the waste products. The chemicals will cross this into the solution through a semi permeable membrane.
>
> In kidney transplantation a healthy kidney is taken from a donor and reattached into the body of the patient. Kidney transplantation has a high success rate.
>
> The major societal issues that accompany these procedures relates to cost. With the current political discussion focused on health care for all individuals there will probably need to be some rationings.
>
> Kidney dialysis is effective but expensive. The procedure takes several hours. Is the benefit to one person from dialysis worth money that could probably benefit many people being treated prophilactially worth it. Many people on dialysis treatment are not good surgical candidates. Should we

use extensive procedures to prolong their lives indefinitely when their quality of life is low?

Even though there is a high rate of success with transplantation there are ethical problems to consider. Tissue typing must be done to ensure the lowest possibility of rejection. Relatives must make hard decisions. If they are a match will they subject themselves to a surgery which may have negative outcomes. If they don't subject themselves to the surgery are they responsible for the death of the person with kidney failure.

Again cost becomes a consideration when considering any type of transplant surgery. This kind of surgery can easily cost well over $100,000. Coupled with the cost of immuno-suppressive medications and possible rejection one must wonder if the cost is justified. Once this type of treatment is started it is also hard to stop. Incessive transplants have higher failure rates. Do we throw good money after bad? Do we limit the number of transplants per person? What is the criteria for selecting the type of person we will allocate this much of our resources to?

Kidney failure means certain death. We have dialysis and transplantation, two effective methods of dealing with it. The future of these two procedures as well as all recent medical advancements will have to be determined after much thoughtful soul searching and debate. To the end our health care system will have to provide the most good for the most people.

Commentary on Sample Response 1

Strengths:

- Very complete and well thought-out
- Uses proper terminology and flows well
- Includes four accurate causes of renal failure
- Describes, in some detail, the dialysis procedure and gives a brief description of transplant technique
- Well-reasoned response to societal effects, both positive and negative

Question 2—Sample Response 2: total score of 4 (out of 5)

These course of kidney failure that may necessitate the use of Dialysis or Kidney transplantation are: a streptococcal infections that results in improper function of the nephrons; Diabetes which causes irritations to the tissues due to increase of glucose levels in blood and inability of the body to properly heal this irritation with resultant occurring of tissue and inability perform the filtering function of the kidney; Hypertension which causes an increase in the pressure in the circulatory structure of the kidneys and ultimately damage the kidney and their filtering function.

Treatment for kidney failure in Dialysis. Dialysis effectively filters the waste products from the blood. It takes over the function of waste management that is usually done by the kidneys. The dialysis patient has a cannula (tubing) inserted usually in the arm or leg. This allows access to the circulatory system without having to enter the artery and vein of the patient each time. Since most dialysis patients receive dialysis as often as three times a week, it is important for easy reliable access to the circulatory system. A needle connected to tubing and this needle is inserted into the cunnula. Blood is withdrawn and sent through the dialysis machine which filters the blood of the waste products by a series of diffusion and active transport processes. The now filtered blood is returned to the patient by a separate tubing and needle inserted into the cannula. This process takes several hours and must be repeated 3 times a week or so.

Another treatment for kidney failure is kidney transplant. A donor kidney is found by testing compatibility; usually a family member. The donor kidney is removed (we each have 2 kidneys so person can live a full life with only one kidney). The diseased kidney is removed form the patient and the new kidney is put in its place. Reconnecting the renal circulatory system and the uretes. Antibiotics & anti rejection drugs are then given.

Implication of these processes to society are far reaching. Dialysis is costly and puts a burden on insurances companies to pay the bills, Medicaid/Medicare to pick up the tab for the uninsured which puts a burden on tax payers. Families are known to put out their whole life savings and end up in long term debt to provide this care for family members. This puts a financial drain on society as a whole. Also, the dialysis patient is not as productive a worker due to treatment times so this effects society.

Kidney transplants are costly as well and often are not covered by insurances as often only the rich can have them unless the patient benefits from special programs or family again go into long term debt. But just done as medication to keep rejection of organ from recurring is life long.

Commentary on Sample Response 2

Strengths:

- A strong answer, covering all parts of the question

Weaknesses:

- Not as thorough a discussion of societal effects as seen in sample 1
- Improper use of the term "active transport"
- Selective membrane inferred, but not stated outright

Question 2—Sample Response 3: total score of 3 (out of 5)

The kidneys are like the filters in a pool. The blood runs through them and the extract the impurities and waste from the blood. If the kidneys are damaged, a person is said to be in renal failure and their blood can become toxic to them.

Failure of the kidneys can results in various ways. First, there may be physical damage to the kidneys through some type of trauma, as in a car accident—Second, their may be biological damage to the kidney through disease such as diabetes, so that organ damage results—Third, a person may have "substandard" kidneys through a genetic defect so that they experience chronic problems with their kidneys.

However, there are two treatments available to those with kidney problems—dialysis and organ transplantation.

In dialysis a patient is hooked up to a dialysis machine which takes the blood from a person through a tube into the machine, the blood is filtered and returned to the patient through a second tube. The dialysis machine is effective in recovering the waste from the blood, but because it is not constant, the patient must undergo treatment 2 to 3 times per week to avoid toxicity—It is also painful and time consuming requiring several hours per treatment.

A second treatment is to have a kidney transplanted from a donor. Because it is in the body, working constantly this is the treatment of choice if at all possible. (A human can survive with one kidney.) A surgical transplant makes dialysis unnecessary.

There are societal issues related to each of the procedures, however.

In dialysis, the treatment is very experience while most would agree that human life is valuable, some question the value on balance with expense. Related also to money is the question "who should pay?" It's hard to make a determination between money and life, but it is a consideration in their times of limited health care dollars. The unfortunate victims in such a balancing would be the elderly who often have limited resources, and shorter life expectancies.

In transplantation, one issue is the short supply of donors because kidneys can be hard to come by. Some ethical issues can arise. "Is it ok to pay privately for an organ?" Should a couple have a second child to harvest a kidney for the first child? If an older person and a younger per both need the kidney, who should get it? Should lifestyle be considered in deciding who gets a kidney?"

These are not easily answered. But they are ones that must be dealt with because both dialysis and transplantation are important and valuable procedures.

Commentary on Sample Response 3

Strengths:

- An adequate answer
  - covers all parts of the question
  - no major omissions or errors

Weaknesses:

- Very general—little use of terminology
- Nothing specific on how dialysis works
  - diffusion
  - selective membranes
- Very skimpy on transplant procedures

Question 2—Sample Response 4: total score of 2 (out of 5)

One cause of kidney failure can be acute trauma to kidney tissue, such as in accident victims. Depending on the extent of the injury, the person can be alleviated by dialysis or replacement (transplantation).

Dialysis is the removal of the metabolic waste products from the blood by machine. The major waste being urea, produces from the metabolism of fatty compounds. Dialysis usually is administered in a hospital, but is now being done increasingly as an outpatient procedure, depending on the severity of the problem. People w/one kidney can go regularly for outpatient dialysis, where those w/complete renal failure are obviously hospitalized.

A transplant of a kidney is the most intensive an light-used option in these situations not only does it involve a major operation and a large-scale in the facility, But require an organ from a person with the same blood types and clotting factor. This is necessary because the person's body accepting the organ will reject the new organ as "Foreign" tissue, rendering the new kidney non functional, unless tissue factors are met.

In either case, the cost to the patient is an economic drain, and quite possibly an emotional one. Society can be affected as well. In the case of transplants, where will the new organs come from? Who decides which person gives an organ away. Donations from dead people (organ donor cards) Are a source, but getting large organs to hospitals in time is a problem.

Commentary on Sample Response 4

Weaknesses:

- Discussion very general and partially incomplete
- Only one cause of kidney failure discussed
- No *science* on dialysis
  - nothing on diffusion and selective membranes
  - nothing on how the procedure is actually done

We will now look at two actual responses to Question 3 and see how the General Scoring Guide was used to rate each response.

Question 3

A region of fixed latitude on a fictional Earthlike planet has the altitude profile shown in the diagram below.

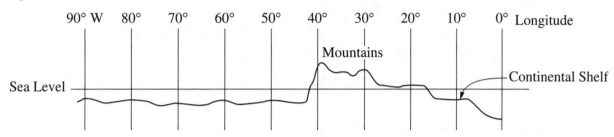

The average value of the acceleration due to gravity on the planet is 5.00 meters per second squared. Over the region depicted in the diagram, the measured values of the acceleration due to gravity are as charted below.

Longitude (°W)	Gravitational Acceleration (m/s^2)
0	5.05
10	5.02
20	4.92
30	4.85
40	4.83
50	5.03
60	5.04
70	5.04
80	5.02
90	5.03

Use the information provided in responding to the following.

(a) What geographic feature corresponds to low values of the acceleration due to gravity? Explain how these factors might be correlated.

(b) Local variations in gravitational acceleration in a region are strongly affected by the density of the rock that underlies it. Assume that there are two main types of rock, X and Y, that make up the planet's bedrock. X is more dense than Y. Referring to the profile above, describe which regions of bedrock are most likely to be made of X and Y, respectively. Explain your reasoning in making these assignments.

(c) For surface locations, at about what longitude would water boil at the lowest temperature? What is the reason for this? (Assume that this planet has an atmosphere.)

Question 3—Sample Response 1: total score of 4 (out of 5)

A) Low values of acceleration due to gravity are associated with higher elevations in the mountains. The acceleration force due to gravity is the attractive force between the masses. It is proportional to the magnitude of the masses and inversely proportional to the square of the distance between the bodies center of mass. (Times the gravitational constant) or $F_g = G\frac{m_1}{m_2}$. In this case, the higher elevations are further from the center of the planet and the acceleration due to gravity is less because of the $1/r^2$ term.

B) The more dense areas would be those with a higher than expected acceleration due to gravity (F_g). The average F_g on the continental shelf is 5.03. Those areas that are higher, and thus rock X are at 60° and 70° longitude. Those at lower F_g and thus rock Y are at 10° and 80° longitude. Noting the variance from shelf to mountains, I would expect 0° longitude to have a higher F_g, thus 0° must be of less dense rock type Y also.

C) Surface location 40° longitude would have water boiling at lowest temperatures. Higher elevations have less atmospheric pressure, hence liquids boil at lower temps. Higher elevations have a shorter "column of air" above them, and thus less psi of atmosphere. The presence of mountains at the 40° latitude will contribute to its low values of acceleration due to gravity. The regions of 20°, 30°, 40° will represent the areas of bedrock made of X because these are areas of lower gravitational acceleration. The regions of 0°, 10°, 50°, 60°, 70°, 80°, 90° represent its areas of bedrock made of Y because these are areas of high gravitational acceleration. Water will boil at a lower temperature at 40° longitude due to lower oxygen content at that level.

Commentary on Sample Response 1

Part (a): This part is done very well. The key point is stated (the farther from Earth's center, the weaker gravity gets); an equation $\left(F_g = G\, m_1\, m_2\, /\, r^2 \right)$ is given in support, as well as a written description of the effect.

Part (b): Correctly notes that differences in elevation must be addressed so that the effect described in part (a) will not be a factor. Then correctly identifies some of the areas with denser rock, but incorrectly identifies a location at 0° longitude as having the less dense rock without taking into account that it is not at the same elevation as the other areas. In areas of the same elevation, the fluctuations should be along the lines of higher g being an indicator of denser rock (denser rock means more mass between the sensor and the center of the planet).

Part (c): Correctly identifies 40° W longitude (the highest altitude) as the spot at which water will have the lowest boiling point. The higher the altitude, the lower the atmospheric pressure. The lower the atmospheric pressure, the lower the boiling point of water. Gives a physical reason for the lower boiling point. A little sketchy but well done.

Question 3—Sample Response 2: total score of 2 (out of 5)

A) The mountains on the surface of the planet contribute to the low acceleration due to gravity. The farther away one is from the center of the planet, the lower the value of acceleration due to gravity.

B) The mountains should be composed of rock Y.
    Let dx = density of rock X
        dy = density of rock Y
         d = mass of rock unit volume

This implies the mass of rock X (mx) is greater than the mass of rock Y (my)

Hence to have of the low values of acceleration in the mountains, it is better to have a mass Y than an or mass X.

Commentary on Sample Response 2:

Part (a): This part is quite sparse. The key point is stated (the farther from Earth's center, the weaker gravity gets), but nothing is given in support.

Part (b): Identifies the same effect as in part (a) as being due to density of rock rather than distance from the center of the planet. Somewhat sketchily identifies higher values of *g* as being indicative of denser rock (denser rock means more mass between the sensor and the center of the planet).

Part (c): No response

We will now look at two actual responses to Question 4 and see how the General Scoring Guide was used to rate each response.

Question 4

The table below summarizes the results of various measurements of the freezing points of a series of samples. Three determinations of freezing point were made for each sample.

Solute Concentration (grams per 100 grams of solvent)	Freezing Point (°C) Trial Number		
	1	2	3
0.0 (pure solvent)	4.6	5.2	4.9
1.0	3.8	3.4	3.6
2.0	2.3	2.7	2.8
4.0	0.6	0.3	2.0

(a) Prepare an appropriate graphical representation of the data.

(b) Do you observe any large discrepancies in the data? If so, where might they come from and how do you interpret them?

(c) Apart from any large discrepancies that might exist, do you observe any small discrepancies in the data? If so, where might they come from and how do you interpret them?

(d) What mathematical relationship between solute concentration and freezing point can be supported by these data? What, if any, additional data would you suggest collecting to support your interpretation of the relationship?

Question 4—Sample Response 1: total score of 4 (out of 5)

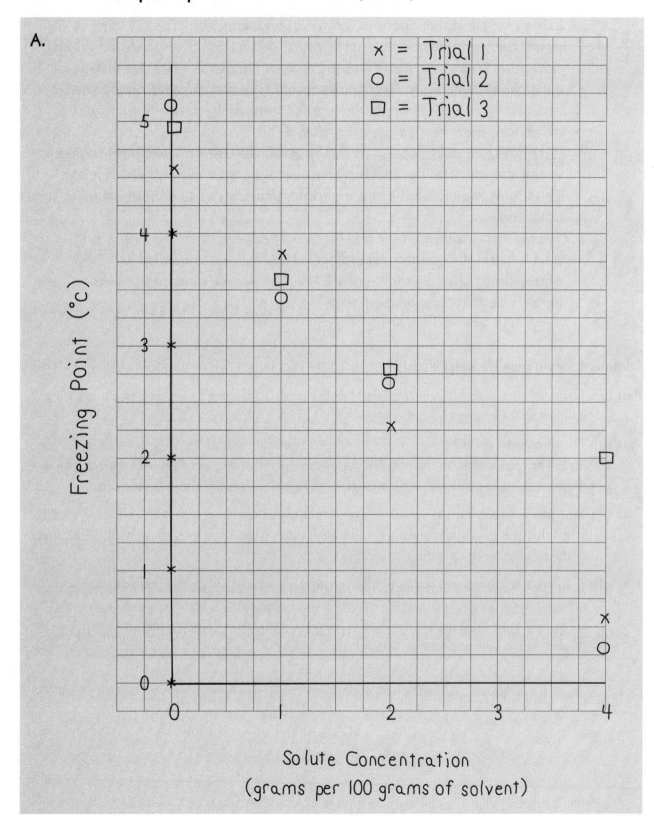

B. The spread of the data appears to be what one might expect with experimental data. There is, however, an exception. The freezing point for the solute concentration of 4 for trial 3 appears to be an outlierile, there is a clear linear trend in the data with this one exception. Personally, I would discount this datum and reject the one trial (trial 3). It might have been caused by faulty equipment or an incorrect solute concentration..

C. With the exception noted in B, the data appear to have a relatively small spread. The spread may be due simply to experimental error. That is, it may indicate the inherent accuracy of the measuring equipment.

D. There is an inverse linear relationship between the Freezing point and the solute concentration, i.e. it can be described by an equation of the form y = -ax + b. Higher solute concentrations would confirm this relationship.

Commentary on Sample Response 1:

Part (a): The graph has correctly calibrated and labeled axes and the points are plotted correctly, but no lines are drawn for the data sets.

Part (b): The discrepant point is correctly distinguished from the normal variation seen in any set of data. The speculation on the cause of the discrepancy and suggested remedy correctly focus on some mistake made rather than on normal variation, which cannot be corrected.

Part (c): This part is vague. Just what is meant by "experimental error" is not clear, and it incorrectly infers that the small discrepancies (normal variation) have something to do with the accuracy of the measuring equipment.

Part (d): The linear relationship is recognized but incorrectly labeled as "inverse" to describe the negative slope. The equation ($y = -ax + b$) is somewhat correct, but the terms (y, a, x, and b) are not identified. (Which is the freezing point, for example?) The confirmatory experiment (higher solute concentrations) was vague.

Question 4—Sample Response 2: total score of 2 (out of 5)

A.

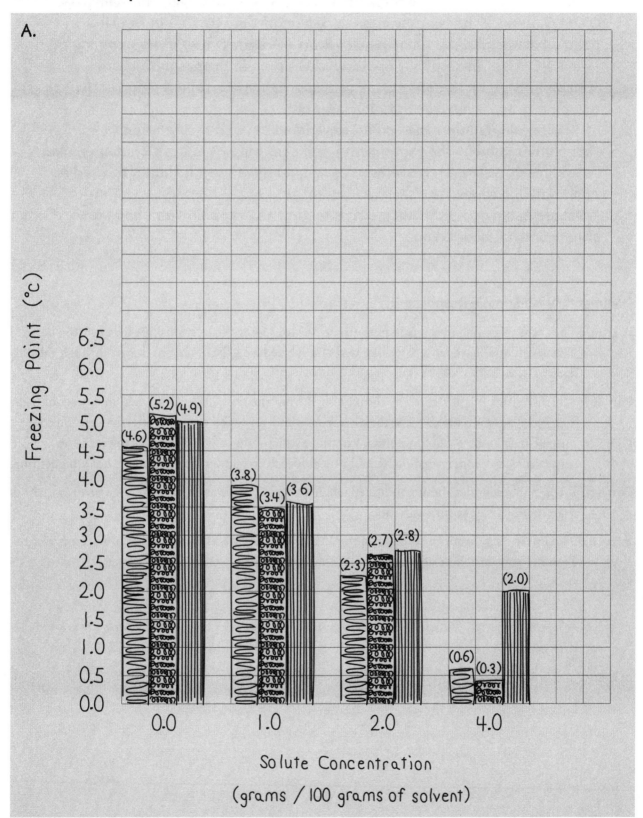

There is significant discrepancy in sample 4.0 trial #3. The samples 0.0, 1.0, and 2.0 have an average variation of only (0.2°C) in freezing points between trials, where as solution 4.0 trial 3 has a discrepancy of over 1.4°C. This discrepancy could be due to an improper mixing or a contamination of the sample or perhaps data was copied incorrectly. The equipment could have been faulty as well.

The small discrepancies could have been caused by transfer techniques used in the experiment, samples may have been contaminated between trials. The thermometer used may have been difficult to read at such small increments.

There seems to be a linear decrease in freezing point as the solute concentration decreased.

Commentary on Sample Response 2

Part (a): The form of graph chosen is inappropriate as it obscures the relationships between the data. The graph does have correctly calibrated and labeled axes. No lines are drawn through related data.

Part (b): The discrepant point is correctly distinguished from the normal variation seen in any set of data. The speculation on the cause of the discrepancy and suggested remedy correctly focus on some mistake made rather than on normal variation, which cannot be corrected. However, the suggested cause, contamination, would probably lead to a lower freezing point, not a higher one.

Part (c): Incorrectly identifies the small discrepancies as having to do with experimental error rather than representing normal variation.

Part (d): The linear relationship is recognized but incorrectly described as a decrease in freezing point as solute concentration decreases (rather than as solute concentration increases).

Chapter 7
Succeeding on the Science Pedagogy Tests

▶ ▶ ▶ ▶ ▶ ▶ ▶ ▶ ▶ ▶ ▶ ▶

The goal of this chapter is to provide you with background information about the development and scoring of the Praxis Science Pedagogy tests along with advice from experts who evaluate test takers' responses. The focus of this advice is to help you understand clearly what a test question is asking and produce a response that demonstrates your knowledge and abilities to the fullest extent. Actual sample questions and student responses, with commentary, will be provided in subsequent chapters to help you formulate a successful answer to the constructed-response question.

How the Tests Are Developed

The *Life Science: Pedagogy* test is designed to measure the subject-area knowledge and competencies necessary for a beginning teacher of biology in a secondary school. Test takers are given a topic for a one-week unit in a high school biology course, followed by a three-part question based on that unit. Test takers are asked to formulate and rationalize learning objectives for the topic and then to describe instructional strategies appropriate for helping students achieve the specific learning objectives, including elements of inquiry-based learning. Furthermore, test takers are asked to describe methods for assessing student mastery of the specific learning objectives. The subject for the instructional unit is drawn from the following content areas: basic principles of science; molecular and cellular biology; classical genetics; evolution; diversity of life, plants, and animals; ecology; and science, technology, and society.

The *Physical Science: Pedagogy* test is designed to measure the knowledge and competencies necessary for a beginning teacher of physical science in a secondary school. Test takers are given a passage of approximately 50 to 150 words that describes a basic topic to be taught in a high school chemistry or physics class. Test takers are asked to identify a science concept important to teach in a high school physical science class and to describe instructional strategies that include elements of inquiry-based learning. Test takers are then asked to describe appropriate assessment methods and a topic for a follow-up lesson. Topics are taken from content common to the physical sciences: matter and energy, heat and thermodynamics, and atomic and nuclear structure.

Both tests assess test takers' ability to understand the principles of lesson design, strategies of instruction, and techniques of assessment and evaluation. This includes knowledge of scientific principles, facts, methodology, philosophy, and the ability to integrate such scientific knowledge.

The test questions are developed by test developers at Educational Testing Service (ETS) and experienced high school and college educators, who also determine acceptable responses. Potential test forms are then field-tested to selected pre-service and beginning teachers at various higher education institutions. In addition to taking the test, the teachers are asked to evaluate the clarity and fairness of the questions. These responses and evaluations are forwarded to the test developers for review and for the final selection of new test forms.

How the Tests Are Scored

As you build your skills in writing answers to pedagogy questions, it is important to keep in mind the process used to score the tests. If you understand the process by which your scores are determined, you may have a better context in which to think about your strategies for success.

After each test administration, test books are returned to ETS. The test booklets in which constructed-response answers are written are sent to the location of the scoring session. The scoring sessions are led by chief scorers. The chief scorer has overall authority over the scoring session and plays a variety of key roles in training and in ensuring consistent and fair scores. All chief scorers and scorers are highly qualified life science or physical science teachers or teacher educators who have many years of experience scoring test questions. An effort is made to balance experienced scorers with newer scorers at each session; the experienced scorers provide continuity with past sessions, and the new scorers ensure that new ideas and perspectives are considered. For the *Physical Science: Pedagogy* test, the scorers consist of physics and chemistry teachers to give breadth and depth of knowledge in the overall field of physical science.

Preparing to train the scorers

Training scorers is a rigorous process, and it is designed to ensure that each response gets a score that is consistent both with the scores given to other papers and with the overall scoring philosophy and criteria established for the test when it was designed.

When a new question is developed, the chief scorers and test developers first review the General Scoring Guide, which contains the overall criteria, stated in general terms, for awarding the appropriate score. They also review and discuss the Question-Specific Scoring Guide, which serves as an application of the general guide to each question on the test. The question-specific guides cannot cover every possible response the scorers will see, but they are designed to give enough examples to guide the scorers in making accurate judgments about the variety of answers they will encounter. The question-specific scoring guides may be modified during the actual scoring sessions as more examples from test takers' responses are discovered and as the input of the other experienced scorers becomes available.

To begin identifying appropriate training materials for an individual question, chief scorers first read through many responses from the first administration of the test to get a sense of the range of answers. They then choose a set of benchmarks, selecting one paper at each score level for each part of the question. These benchmarks serve as solid representative examples of the kind of response that meets the scoring criteria at each score level and are considered the foundation for score standards throughout the administration of the specific test question. For some tests, the benchmark papers are not always immediately available because the pool of responses is small. Therefore, benchmarks may be identified over more than one test administration. Different benchmarks are selected for each test form administered.

The chief scorer then chooses a larger set of test-taker responses to serve as sample papers, or "training papers." These training papers represent the wide variety of possible responses that the scorers might see. The training papers serve as the basis for practice scoring at the scoring session, so that the scorers can rehearse how they will apply the scoring criteria before they begin unaided scoring. After the chief scorer is done with his or her selections and discussions, the sets they have chosen are photocopied and inserted into the scorers' folders in preparation for the session.

Training at the main scoring session

In general, for each question, the training session proceeds in the following way:

1. All scorers carefully read through the question they will be scoring.

2. All scorers review the General Scoring Guide and the Question-Specific Scoring Guide for the question.

3. The chief scorer guides the scorers through the set of benchmark responses for that question, explaining in detail why each response received the score it did. Scorers are encouraged to ask questions and share their perspectives.

4. Scorers then practice on the set of sample training papers chosen by the chief scorer. The chief scorer polls the scorers on what scores they awarded and then leads a discussion to ensure that there is a consensus about the scoring criteria and how they are to be applied.

5. When the chief scorer is confident that the scorers for that question will apply the criteria consistently and accurately, the actual scoring begins.

Quality-control processes

A number of procedures are followed to ensure that accuracy of scoring is maintained during the scoring session. Most importantly, each response is scored twice, with the first scorer's decision hidden from the second scorer. The chief scorer evaluates the scores given by the two scorers. If the two scores for a part of the question are the same or differ by only one point, the scoring for that part is considered complete and the examinee will be awarded the sum of the two scores. If the two scores differ by more than one point, the response is scored by the chief scorer. If this third score is midway between the first two scores, the test takers's score for the question is the sum of the first two scores; otherwise, it is the sum of the third score and whichever of the first two scores is closer to it.

Another way of maintaining scoring accuracy is through back-reading. Throughout the session, the chief scorer checks random samples of scores awarded by all the scorers. If the chief scorer finds that a scorer is not applying the scoring criteria appropriately, that scorer is given more training.

The entire scoring process—general and specific scoring guides, standardized benchmarks and samples, consensus scoring, adjudication procedures, back-reading, and rotation of test questions to a variety of scorers—is applied consistently and systematically at every scoring session to ensure comparable scores for each administration and across all administrations of the test.

Advice from the experts

Scorers who have scored thousands of real tests offer the following practical pieces of advice.

1. **Read and answer the question accurately.** Be sure to dissect the parts of the question and analyze what each part is asking you to do. If the question asks you to *describe* or *discuss,* keep those requirements in mind when composing your response—do not just give a list. Keep in mind that the lesson you are describing is intended for a high school level course.

2. **Answer everything that is being asked in the question.** This seems simple, but many test takers fail to provide a complete response. If a question asks you to do three distinct things in your response, don't give a response to just two of those things. No matter how well you write about those two things, the scorers will not award you full credit for that part. It is essential that you include a rationale for the appropriateness and effectiveness of an activity or assessment in your response.

3. **Give a thorough and detailed response.** Your response must indicate to the scorers that you have a thorough understanding of the applicable life or physical science principles and guidelines. The scorers will not read anything into your response that is not expressly written. If something is not written, they do not know that you know it and will not give you credit for it.

4. **Limit the breadth of the lesson you choose.** A response is generally stronger when it is fully detailed as described above. This often means it is better to discuss one lesson topic more fully, than a number of topics more generally.

5. **Do not change the question or challenge the basis of the question.** Stay focused on the question that is asked. You will receive no credit if you choose to answer another question or indicate that what the question is asking is inappropriate.

6. **Be sure to link your responses logically.** A well-planned assessment activity must link strongly to the lesson presented. A well-designed follow-up lesson must have a strong logical link to the initial lesson. Be sure that these points are clearly covered in your response.

7. **Number each part of your response.** Numbering your responses enhances the scoring process; however, scorers will give the test taker every advantage in awarding score points. For example, if a response inadvertently includes part of an answer to part 2 under part 3, the points will be awarded to part 2.

General Scoring Guides

Life Science: Pedagogy (0234)

The following general guide provides the rubrics for scoring the constructed-response questions on the *Life Science: Pedagogy* test.

The question in this test consists of three parts. While the test is read as a whole and answers in one part of a test may be dependent on answers in other parts of the test, each part receives an individual score. All parts are equally weighted and are scored according to the rubrics in the General Scoring Guide below, on a scale of 0 to 5.

<u>Score</u>	<u>Comment</u>
5	Demonstrates a *superior* understanding of how to teach the science concepts required by the question by providing well-reasoned explanations and using accurate scientific terminology in responding to all three parts of the prompt.
4	Demonstrates a *strong* understanding of how to teach the science concepts required by the question by providing logical explanations and using accurate scientific terminology in responding to all three parts of the prompt.
3	Demonstrates an *adequate* understanding of how to teach the science concepts required by the question by providing generally clear and logical explanations and by using fairly accurate scientific terminology in responding to all three parts of the prompt.
2	Demonstrates a *limited* understanding of how to teach the science concepts required by the question.
1	Demonstrates a *very limited* understanding of how to teach the science concepts required by the question.
0	Blank, completely inaccurate, inappropriate, or off topic.

Physical Science: Pedagogy (0483)

The following general guide provides the rubrics for scoring the constructed-response questions on the *Physical Science: Pedagogy* test.

Since this test consists of a series of related parts, a test taker's response is scored by rating each part individually. All parts are scored according to the scoring rubric below, on a scale of 0 to 5.

Part 1 of the question serves to help the test taker communicate effectively to the scorers the topic chosen for part 2 and to help the test taker focus on a specific topic. *The responses for parts 1 and 2 are scored together. The response to parts 1 and 2 combined counts for 50% of the overall score, and the responses to parts 3 and 4 count for 25% each.*

Parts 1 and 2 combined, INSTRUCTIONAL STRATEGIES and ACTIVITIES, will be scored according to the following scoring rubrics.

Score	Comment
5	Demonstrates a ***superior*** understanding of how to plan a physical science lesson, as evidenced by the following:

- shows evidence of a very good understanding of science content by using accurate language, graphs, equations, etc., appropriately in context with very good integration of concepts

- provides a fully detailed description of instructional strategies and activities that include elements of inquiry-based learning and are appropriate for teaching the lesson

- presents a lesson with a logical and definite structure

- provides a clear and logical explanation of why the instructional strategies and activities would be appropriate and effective

4	Demonstrates a ***strong*** understanding of how to plan a physical science lesson, as evidenced by the following:

- shows evidence of a good understanding of science content by using accurate language, graphs, equations, etc., appropriately in context

- describes in some detail instructional strategies and activities that include elements of inquiry-based learning and are appropriate for teaching the lesson

- presents a lesson with definite structure

- provides a brief but logical explanation of why the instructional strategies and activities would be appropriate and effective

3	Demonstrates an ***adequate*** understanding of how to plan a physical science lesson, as evidenced by the following:

- shows evidence of an adequate understanding of science content (including no major inaccuracies)

- provides a description of an instructional strategy and an activity that include elements of inquiry-based learning and are appropriate for teaching the lesson

- provides some evidence of structure in the lesson

- may or may **not** provide an explanation of why the instructional strategies and activities would be appropriate and effective

2   Demonstrates *limited* understanding of how to plan a physical science lesson, as evidenced by one or more of the following:

- shows evidence of a limited understanding of science content (possibly including major inaccuracies)

- provides a limited description of an instructional strategy or activity appropriate for teaching the lesson

- provides very limited evidence of structure in the lesson

1   Demonstrates *little or no* understanding of how to plan a physical science lesson, as evidenced by one or more of the following:

- shows evidence of poor understanding of science content

- may provide a vague or superficial description of an instructional strategy or activity appropriate for teaching the lesson

- provides no evidence of structure in the lesson

0   Completely inaccurate or inappropriate, blank, or off topic

Part 3, ASSESSMENT, will be scored according to the following scoring rubrics.

Score	Comment

5   Demonstrates a *superior* understanding of how to plan an assessment activity, as evidenced by the following:

- provides a fully detailed description of an assessment activity appropriate for teaching the lesson

- provides a clear and logical explanation of why the assessment activity is appropriate and effective

4   Demonstrates a *strong* understanding of how to plan an assessment activity, as evidenced by the following:

- provides a detailed description of an assessment activity appropriate for teaching the lesson

- provides a logical explanation of why the assessment activity is appropriate and effective

3   Demonstrates an *adequate* understanding of how to plan an assessment activity, as evidenced by the following:

- provides a detailed description of an assessment activity appropriate for teaching the lesson

- may or may **not** provide an explanation of why the assessment activity is appropriate and effective

2   Demonstrates *limited* understanding of how to plan an assessment activity, as evidenced by one or more of the following:

- provides a limited description of an assessment activity appropriate for teaching the lesson

1   Demonstrates *little or no* understanding of how to plan an assessment activity, as evidenced by one or more of the following:

- may provide a vague or superficial description of an appropriate assessment activity related to the lesson

0   Completely inaccurate or inappropriate, blank, or off topic

Part 4, FOLLOW-UP, will be scored according to the following scoring rubrics.

Score	Comment

5   Demonstrates a *superior* understanding of how to plan a follow-up lesson, as evidenced by the following:

- clearly identifies and provides a fully detailed description of a topic for a follow-up lesson appropriate to build on the first lesson

- provides a clear and logical explanation of why the topic for the follow-up lesson is appropriate and effective

4   Demonstrates a *strong* understanding of how to plan a follow-up lesson, as evidenced by the following:

- clearly identifies and provides a detailed description of a topic for a follow-up lesson appropriate to build on the first lesson

- provides a logical explanation of why the topic for the follow-up lesson is appropriate and effective

3   Demonstrates an *adequate* understanding of how to plan a follow-up lesson, as evidenced by the following:

- identifies and provides a description of a topic for a follow-up lesson appropriate to build on the first lesson

- may or may **not** provide an explanation of why the follow-up lesson is appropriate and effective

2   Demonstrates *limited* understanding of how to plan a follow-up lesson, as evidenced by one or more of the following:

- provides a limited description of a topic for a follow-up lesson appropriate to build on the first lesson

1   Demonstrates *little or no* understanding of how to plan a follow-up lesson, as evidenced by one or more of the following:

- provides a vague or superficial description of a topic for a follow-up lesson related to the first lesson

0   Completely inaccurate or inappropriate, blank, or off topic

Question-Specific Scoring Guide

After a question is developed, three or four knowledgeable experts develop ideas for model answers. These model answers are used to develop a Question-Specific Scoring Guide (QSSG), which creates a list of specific examples that would receive various scores for each part of the test question. This list contains examples of various answers, not *all* possible answers. These guides provide the basis for choosing the papers that serve as the benchmarks and sample papers used for training the scorers at the scoring session. It also helps scorers assign points during the actual scoring session.

So how does a scorer know to assign 3 out of 5 points on part 1, or 4 out of 5 points on part 2? The scorer reads the question and determines which parts of the question have been answered and how well each one is addressed. Below are examples of how points are assigned for specific parts of the test using the QSSG:

Part	Score	Comment
1—Objectives	3	States three distinct, relevant learning objectives OR states three relevant but overlapping objectives.
		For each objective, provides a limited to generally clear explanation of their importance.
		For each objective, provides some main ideas and skills covered by each objective.
2—Instructional Strategies	4	Provides a detailed description of appropriate instructional strategies that would help students meet all three objectives identified in Part 1.
		Strategies include one or more examples of inquiry-based learning.

Strategies include a description of a laboratory exercise.

The test taker states and makes good use of the 90-minute session for purposes other than summary evaluation.

Given the information above about how constructed-responses are scored and what the scorers are looking for in successful responses, you are now ready to look at specific questions, suggestions on how to approach the questions, and sample responses and scores given to those responses.

Chapter 8
Preparing for the Science Pedagogy Tests

► ► ► ► ► ► ► ► ► ► ► ►

The goal of this chapter is to provide you with strategies for reading, analyzing, and understanding the questions on the Science Pedagogy tests, and for outlining and writing successful responses.

Introduction to the Tests

The pedagogy tests in life science and physical science are intended to assess how well you are able to plan, design, and assess a specific lesson in the field of life science or physical science. The *Life Science: Pedagogy* test is composed of one three-part constructed-response question. The first part of the question asks you to summarize the content areas that will be covered in the unit, including the main ideas and skills you would expect your students to know. Next, you will be required to develop diverse, engaging, and level-appropriate instructional strategies for the content areas you've selected. Finally, you will be asked to detail end-of-unit assessment tools that will help you determine student mastery of the unit's main ideas and skills.

The *Physical Science: Pedagogy* test is composed of one four-part constructed-response question. Part 1 of the question requires you to identify a specific topic to be the focus of a lesson from a broad unit. This part of the question should be answered concisely since it is scored with part 2. For part 2 of the question, you will be required to develop a lesson plan and describe instructional strategies and classroom activities for the lesson. This part of the response must include elements of inquiry-based learning. Part 3 of the question asks you to detail and justify an appropriate and effective assessment technique that will help determine students' learning and the teacher's effectiveness. Part 4 of the question asks you to identify and describe a follow-up lesson that is built on the lesson described in part 2 of the response.

What to Study

Life Science: Pedagogy test

Success on this test is not simply a matter of learning more about how to respond to constructed-response questions. Success on the test also requires subject area knowledge and awareness of current and appropriate pedagogical and assessment techniques. Therefore, it would serve you well to review texts and notes relevant to the test's subject matter. The following books and Web sites are particularly relevant to the type of material covered by the test. (Note: The test is not based on these resources, and they do not necessarily cover every topic that may be included in the test.)

Campbell, Neil A., and Jane B. Reece. *Biology*, 6th ed. Benjamin Cummings, 2002.

> This book provides in-depth coverage of key concepts in biology at a level understandable by any test taker who has completed an introductory biology course at the college level. In addition to studying the specific material within each chapter, briefly review the key objectives presented and

the organization of the chapters. In most cases, each chapter contains material suitable for a one-week instructional unit.

Any other college-level general biology text would also be suitable for review.

Tillery, Bill W., Eldon D. Enger, and Frederick C. Ross. *Integrated Science*, 2nd ed. McGraw-Hill Higher Education, 2003.

This book provides a simplified overview of important life sciences content areas.

National Resource Council. *National Science Education Standards*. National Academy Press, 1996.

This document summarizes the standards for science teaching, science content, and assessment.

Bybee, Rodger W., Janet Carlson Powell, and Leslie W. Trowbridge, *Teaching Secondary School Science: Strategies for Developing Scientific Literacy*, 7th ed. Merrill-Prentice Hall, 1999.

Carin, Arthur A., and Joel E. Bass. *Teaching Science as Inquiry*, 9th ed. Prentice Hall, Inc., 2001.

Chiapetta, Eugene L., and Thomas R. Koballa. *Science Instruction in the Middle and Secondary Schools*, 5th ed. Merrill-Prentice Hall, 2002.

These texts provide an introduction to and examples of current pedagogical strategies in secondary school science.

www.project2061.org/

This Web site connects to the home page for Project 2061. Project 2061 is an initiative in which the American Association for the Advancement of Science is working to reform K-12 science, mathematics, and technology education nationwide.

www.mcrel.org/compendium/Standard.asp?SubjectID=2

This Web site reviews national science standards and novel instructional methods appropriate for secondary school-level life sciences.

www.nsta.org

This Web site links to the National Science Teachers Association and includes many useful tools for science instruction at all levels.

Physical Science: Pedagogy test

There are two basic areas that a student should consider reviewing to score well on the *Physical Science: Pedagogy* test. These areas are content and pedagogy (lesson development and planned instruction).

Content

It is essential that those who plan to teach the physical sciences be rooted firmly in the content material. Although the major focus of the pedagogy test is not the content, a thorough understanding of the content will enhance strong lesson planning and assessment. Preparation for the content required in this test would be covered in many general chemistry and introductory physics courses. These courses typically are offered during the first and second years of college. It will serve you well to review texts and notes relevant to the test's subject matter.

Pedagogy Information

1. **Review your own experience as a student of physical science.**

   - Consider why you want to teach physical science.

     □ What links have you made in your mind between the concepts to be taught?

     □ Devise models, experiments, and graphic organizers that could be used to teach these topics.

     □ Review your notes from past courses with the intent of seeing what techniques your instructors used.

   - These concepts have been in the curriculum for many years.

     □ What demonstrations, experiments, and lessons have you seen that were worthwhile?

     □ How did the instructors incorporate elements of inquiry learning into their lessons?

   - Review your lessons from your teaching methods course.

     □ How are lessons planned and implemented?

     □ What are the essential features of a good lesson?

     □ How do you engage students in the learning?

2. **Use the Internet as a resource.** Frequently, experienced teachers share their lessons online. Many of these lessons are creative and well worth modeling for starting teachers. The lessons you review may include an activity or demonstration that could be used in your response to show how you might engage students.

3. **Review current educational literature related to physical science and pedagogy.** The inquiry method is a topic that is widely written about in educational journals. Be sure to have a good understanding of what an inquiry lesson involves, since the highest scores on the test will incorporate elements of inquiry, as designated in the scoring guide. Keep in mind that you should not recommend or permit any learning activities that may be unsafe.

4. **Familiarize yourself with the scoring guide.** That should allow you to maximize your time during the actual test taking. Know the criteria for a good score from the General Scoring Guide and base your response on those criteria.

5. **Write several short essays and have them reviewed.** Choose several topics from the list of content options and write a number of essays. Follow the scoring guide from chapter 7. Write your essay within the one-hour time frame of the test. Have an experienced teacher of physical science critique your work and make suggestions. Ask him or her to use the scoring guide when reviewing your work. Start with topics you feel stronger with, but then progress to ones that will be more of a challenge.

Writing a Successful Response to a Question

Understanding what the questions are asking

It is impossible to write a successful response to a question unless you thoroughly understand the question. Often test takers jump into their written response without taking enough time to analyze exactly what the question is asking and how many different parts of the question need to be addressed. The time you invest in making sure you understand what the question is asking and in outlining your answer will very likely pay off in a better score.

To illustrate the importance of understanding the question before you begin writing, let's start with a sample question in life science:

You will be teaching a one-week unit on the cell for a first-year high school biology course. Assume that your class meets five times a week in four 45-minute sessions and one 90-minute session. Based on this information, provide detailed responses to all sections of the following three parts of the question.

Part 1—Content and Rationale

Discuss each of the following:

- State three significant learning objectives for the unit on the cell that you would like your students to achieve. These should be major concepts crucial to an understanding of the cell and appropriate for a high school biology course.

- Explain why it is important to concentrate on each of these objectives.

- Describe the main ideas and skills you would expect students to learn.

Part 2—Instructional Strategies

Describe in detail the instructional strategies you would use during the week to help your students achieve the three learning objectives you identified in part 1. Include elements of inquiry-based learning in these strategies.

Part 3—Assessment

Discuss each of the following:

- Describe in detail two distinct methods of assessment (excluding multiple-choice) that are appropriate to use as an end-of-unit evaluation to measure how well your students have achieved the three learning objectives.

- Describe specific examples of acceptable projects and/or responses you would expect from the students and the criteria you would use in evaluating them.

- Explain how each of these methods of assessment will provide information about student knowledge and skills.

Key components of the question

✓ The question is asking you to design a comprehensive curriculum unit related to "the cell."

✓ You are asked to provide a level-appropriate response—your target audience is a first-year high school general biology class.

✓ You are given specific time guidelines (one week, or 270 minutes) in which to complete in-class instruction and assessment. You may assume, as in a typical high school class, that students can complete some assignments outside of class time.

✓ There are *three* parts to the question.

✓ Part 1 requires *three* components for a complete response:
   □ State *three* distinct, significant, and appropriate learning objectives related to the cell.
   □ Provide justification for your selection of these objectives.
   □ Provide a description of main ideas and skills for *each* objective.

✓ Part 2 requires a detailed summary of important instructional strategies to guide student learning for *each* objective.

✓ One or more instructional strategies should include inquiry-based learning.

✓ Part 3 requires *four* components for a complete response:
   □ Describe *two* techniques that will assess student understanding of *each* objective.
   □ Provide examples of specific questions or projects you would assign and describe responses or the finished product that you would expect from a student for *each* technique.
   □ State grading criteria for *each* technique—such as developing a grading rubric.
   □ Provide justification for your selection of *each* assessment tool—explain why each technique is a suitable assessment tool.

✓ Assessment techniques should be end-of-unit, not ongoing, in design.

✓ Assessment techniques cannot be multiple-choice. This includes alternate versions of multiple-choice, such as true/false and matching.

Organizing your response

Successful responses start with successful planning, either with an outline or with another form of notes. By planning your response, you greatly decrease the chances that you will forget to answer any part of the question. You increase the chances of creating a well-organized response, which is what the scorers look for. Space is provided in the test booklet for you to outline your answer prior to writing your final response. If you choose to complete an outline, budget your time wisely! The scorers will not give credit for work done in the "notes" section of the test booklet. It is also important to understand that each of the three parts of the *Life Science: Pedagogy* test question is worth an equal number of points. This means that you should develop your response to all three parts equally well.

To illustrate a possible strategy for planning a response, let us focus again on the sample question introduced in the previous section. We analyzed the question and found that it necessitated a three-part response. You might begin by jotting down those parts on your notes page, leaving space under each. This will ensure that you address each part when you begin writing.

Sample Notes 1—Main parts to be answered

Part I -   Objective 1

Objective 2

Objective 3

Part II -   Objective 1 Instructional strategies

Objective 2 Instructional strategies

Objective 3 Instructional strategies

Part III - Assessment technique 1

Assessment technique 2

These are key characteristics that the scorers will look for:

- Answer all parts of the question.
- Give reasons for your answers.
- Demonstrate subject-specific knowledge in your answer.

With these characteristics in mind, you then might quickly fill out the components you want to address in each part, like this:

Sample Notes 2—Components under each main part

Part I - Objective 1

Justification

Main ideas and skills

Objective 2

Justification

Main ideas and skills

Objective 3

Justification

Main ideas and skills

Part II - Objective 1 Instructional strategies

Objective 2 Instructional strategies

Objective 3 Instructional strategies

Part III - Assessment technique 1 (covering objective(s) #___)

Specific questions, projects, etc.

Expected responses, product, etc.

Grading criteria

Justification

Assessment technique 2 (covering objective(s) #___)

Specific questions, projects, etc.

Expected responses, product, etc.

Grading criteria

Justification

Finally, it's time to outline the specific scientific details, pedagogy, and assessment tools.

Sample Notes 3—Adding details

Part I -   Objective 1: Cell Theory
    Justification:
        - cell is basic unit of life
        - cell classification
    Main ideas and skills
        - characteristics of living cells
        - compare prokaryotes vs. eukaryotes
        - historical figures

Objective 2: Cell Structure and Function
    Justification:
        - structure-function relationships are key theme in biology
        - understand basic functions that all living organisms must carry out
    Main ideas and skills
        - know key components of all cells (organelles, membranes, genetic material, etc.)
        - know the functions of each component
        - identify components using microscope and diagrams
        - recognize plants vs. animals based on organelle types

Objective 3: Cell reproduction
    Justification:
        - relate to cell theory
        - importance to wound healing, propagation

Main ideas and skills:

- stages of mitosis and meiosis

Part II - Objective 1 Instructional strategies

introductory lecture

text search to find one historical figure in cell biology, students share results

Objective 2 Instructional strategies—use 90 min. session here

lab - teaches use of microscope and slide preparation, identify organelles visible via light microscopy

compare plant vs. animal cells

demo - membrane transport specificity

video - show electron micrograph images of organelles

inquiry - break students into groups to study diseases caused by abnormal function of one organelle. Assign a different disease to each group and ask them to predict what would be wrong with diseased person, then do Internet research to find out what the answer is, share with class

Objective 3 Instructional strategies

lecture

lab - microscope slides of mitosis/meiosis stages

Part III - Assessment technique 1 (covering objective(s) # 1 and 2): Essay test

Specific questions, projects, etc.

Give several examples of essay questions

Expected responses, product, etc.

Grading criteria

Justification

Assessment technique 2 (covering objective(s) #2 and 3): Lab Practicum

    Specific questions, projects, etc.

    Give examples of review and never before seen slides, diagrams, etc., on practicum

    Expected responses, product, etc.

    Grading criteria

    Justification

You have now created the skeleton of your written response.

Writing your response

Now the important step of writing your response begins. Remember that the scorers will not consider your notes when they score your paper, so it is crucial that you integrate all the important ideas from your notes into your actual written response.

Some test takers believe that every written response on a Praxis™ test has to be in formal essay form—that is, with an introductory paragraph, then paragraphs with the response to the question, then a concluding paragraph. This is the case for very few Praxis tests (e.g., *English* and *Writing*). The Science Pedagogy tests do not require formal essays, so you should use techniques that allow you to communicate information efficiently and clearly. For example, you may supplement your answer with bulleted or numbered lists, charts, or diagrams. Also, if you organize your answer effectively, you don't waste time rewriting elements of the question within your answer. Keep in mind that you should avoid the use of undefined acronyms, for example, K-W-L chart of 5E's.

Returning to our sample question, note in the following sample response how the outline of the response to part 1 of the question can be transformed into the final written response. (This is an actual response by a test taker who received a score of 3 out of 5 points for part 1.)

Part 1 - Three objectives for the unit. Explain the importance of each of these objectives. Describe main ideas and skills I expect the students to learn.

1. The students will be able to recognize the difference between prokaryotes and eukaryotes/Cell theory. The understanding of the difference between prokaryotic and eukaryotic cells is very important for the classification of cells based on the presence of a nucleus. It is essential for the understanding of when each specific cell came to be and how larger animals are made up of a specific kind of cells. Included in this objective is the learning of the cell theory. The students need to understand that anything living or once was alive is made up of cells. And that all cells come from other living cells. There is no spontaneous generation like scientists in the past had thought.

2. The students will be able to recognize the structures (organelles) of both plant and animal cells. They will also have an understanding of the function of each cell structure. It is important that each student can recognize what each structure looks like and what each structure is responsible for doing to keep the cell functional. It is also important that each student (when given a chance) can locate specific structures of the cell when viewed through the microscope. When the students understand what the structures look like then they can start to understand how all the structures work together to keep organisms alive. Students will be expected to name all the structures and their functions.

3. The student will understand how cells reproduce. It is important that the students understand that cells come from other living cells. The methods that are important are mitosis and meiosis. The students will understand the 5 stages of mitosis and compare the stages to the sexual reproduction stages of meiosis. These concepts are important for the understanding of wound healing and propagation of species. Students will be expected to identify specific stages in mitosis when seen through a microscope.

Whatever format you select, the important thing is that your answer needs to be thorough, complete, and detailed. Additional examples of test questions and student responses are presented in chapter 10.

Chapter 9

Practice Questions—Science Pedagogy Tests

▶ ▶ ▶ ▶ ▶ ▶ ▶ ▶ ▶ ▶ ▶ ▶

Now that you have worked through strategies and preparation for taking the Science Pedagogy tests, you should answer the following practice questions. These questions are actual test questions, now retired. You will probably find it helpful to simulate actual testing conditions, giving yourself 60 minutes to work on each of the questions. You can use the lined answer pages provided if you wish.

Keep in mind that the test you take at an actual administration will have different questions. You should not expect your level of performance to be exactly the same as when you take the test at an actual administration, since numerous factors affect a person's performance in any given testing situation.

When you have finished the practice questions, you can read through the sample responses with scorer annotations in chapter 10.

THE PRAXIS SERIES
Professional Assessments for Beginning Teachers®

Educational Testing Service

TEST NAME:

Life Science: Pedagogy (0234)
Physical Science: Pedagogy (0483)

Time—120 Minutes

2 Questions

NO CALCULATORS PERMITTED

LIFE SCIENCE: PEDAGOGY

Question

Time—60 minutes

You will be teaching a one-week unit on the cell for a first-year high school biology course. Assume that your class meets five times a week in four 45-minute sessions and one 90-minute session. Based on this information, provide detailed responses to all sections of the following three parts of the question.

Part 1—Content and Rationale

Discuss each of the following:

- State three significant learning objectives for the unit on the cell that you would like your students to achieve. These should be major concepts crucial to an understanding of the cell and appropriate for a high school biology course.

- Explain why it is important to concentrate on each of these objectives.

- Describe the main ideas and skills you would expect students to learn.

Part 2—Instructional Strategies

Describe in detail the instructional strategies you would use during the week to help your students achieve the three learning objectives you identified in part 1. Include elements of inquiry-based learning in these strategies.

Part 3—Assessment

Discuss each of the following:

- Describe in detail two distinct methods of assessment (excluding multiple-choice) that are appropriate to use as an end-of-unit evaluation to measure how well your students have achieved the three learning objectives.

- Describe specific examples of acceptable projects and/or responses you would expect from the students and the criteria you would use in evaluating them.

- Explain how each of these methods of assessment will provide information about student knowledge and skills.

NOTES

PHYSICAL SCIENCE: PEDAGOGY

Question

Time—60 minutes

You are planning to teach a unit on radioactivity to a high school physical science class. Read the passage below and use the information to help you respond to parts 1, 2, 3, and 4 below.

> Radioactivity refers to the spontaneous transformation of an unstable atomic nucleus by the emission of radiation and/or particles. A specific transformation may occur within a time frame ranging from less than a microsecond to greater than billions of years. Each radioactive element has a particular mode, or modes, of decay, such as alpha, beta, and gamma decay.

1. Identify a major concept directly related to the topic of radioactivity as described in the paragraph above around which you will develop a lesson for a high school physical science class.

2. Describe the instructional strategies and classroom activities you would use to open, develop, and close this lesson. Include elements of inquiry-based learning in these strategies and activities. Explain why you think your strategies and activities would be appropriate and effective.

3. Describe in detail an appropriate assessment activity you would use in conjunction with this lesson. Explain why you think this activity would be appropriate and effective.

4. Identify and describe in detail a topic you would use for a follow-up lesson to build on this lesson. Explain why this topic would be appropriate and effective for a follow-up lesson.

NOTES

Begin your response to *Life Science: Pedagogy* question here.

(*Life Science: Pedagogy* question—*Continued*)

_____

_____

_____

_____

_____

_____

_____

_____

_____

_____

_____

_____

_____

_____

_____

_____

_____

_____

_____

_____

_____

_____

(*Life Science: Pedagogy* question—*Continued*)

_____

_____

_____

_____

_____

_____

_____

_____

_____

_____

_____

_____

_____

_____

_____

_____

_____

_____

_____

_____

(*Life Science: Pedagogy* question—*Continued*)

_____

_____

_____

_____

_____

_____

_____

_____

_____

_____

_____

_____

_____

_____

_____

_____

_____

_____

_____

_____

Begin your response to *Physical Science: Pedagogy* question here.

(*Physical Science: Pedagogy* question—*Continued*)

_____

_____

_____

_____

_____

_____

_____

_____

_____

_____

_____

_____

_____

_____

_____

_____

_____

_____

_____

_____

_____

(*Physical Science: Pedagogy* question—*Continued*)

_____

_____

_____

_____

_____

_____

_____

_____

_____

_____

_____

_____

_____

_____

_____

_____

_____

_____

_____

_____

_____

_____

_____

_____

_____

_____

(*Physical Science: Pedagogy* question—*Continued*)

_____

_____

_____

_____

_____

_____

_____

_____

_____

_____

_____

_____

_____

_____

_____

_____

_____

_____

_____

_____

_____

_____

_____

_____

Chapter 10

Sample Responses and How They Were Scored—
Science Pedagogy Tests

▶   ▶   ▶   ▶   ▶   ▶   ▶   ▶   ▶   ▶   ▶   ▶

This chapter presents actual sample responses to the practice test questions and explanations for the scores they received.

As discussed in chapter 8, the question on the *Life Science: Pedagogy* test is scored in three parts. Each part is scored on a scale of 0 to 5, with the total number of points being 15. The question on the *Physical Science: Pedagogy* test is also scored in three parts. Parts 1 and 2 combined, part 3, and part 4 of the response will each be scored on a scale of 0 to 5. Parts 1 and 2 combined are worth 50 percent of the total score, and parts 3 and 4 are each worth 25 percent of the total score, with the total number of points from each scorer being 20. The final scaled score is determined on the basis of how the test taker's point total ranks in comparison with standards set by Educational Testing Service (ETS). The final scaled score needed to pass the test is determined by the test taker's individual state or certification agency.

Life Science: Pedagogy Test

The practice test question and a summary of the General Scoring Guide are restated below.

Question

Time—60 minutes

You will be teaching a one-week unit on the cell for a first-year high school biology course. Assume that your class meets five times a week in four 45-minute sessions and one 90-minute session. Based on this information, provide detailed responses to all sections of the following three parts of the question.

Part 1—Content and Rationale

Discuss each of the following:

- State three significant learning objectives for the unit on the cell that you would like your students to achieve. These should be major concepts crucial to an understanding of the cell and appropriate for a high school biology course.

- Explain why it is important to concentrate on <u>each</u> of these objectives.

- Describe the main ideas and skills you would expect students to learn.

Part 2—Instructional Strategies

Describe in detail the instructional strategies you would use during the week to help your students achieve the three learning objectives you identified in part 1. Include elements of inquiry-based learning in these strategies.

Part 3—Assessment

Discuss each of the following:

- Describe in detail two distinct methods of assessment (excluding multiple-choice) that are appropriate to use as an end-of-unit evaluation to measure how well your students have achieved the three learning objectives.

- Describe specific examples of acceptable projects and/or responses you would expect from the students and the criteria you would use in evaluating them.

- Explain how each of these methods of assessment will provide information about student knowledge and skills.

General Scoring Guide

Score	Comment
5	Demonstrates a *superior* understanding of how to teach the science concepts required by the question by providing well-reasoned explanations and using accurate scientific terminology in responding to all three parts of the prompt.
4	Demonstrates a *strong* understanding of how to teach the science concepts required by the question by providing logical explanations and using accurate scientific terminology in responding to all three parts of the prompt.
3	Demonstrates an *adequate* understanding of how to teach the science concepts required by the question by providing generally clear and logical explanations and by using fairly accurate scientific terminology in responding to all three parts of the prompt.
2	Demonstrates a *limited* understanding of how to teach the science concepts required by the question.
1	Demonstrates a *very limited* understanding of how to teach the science concepts required by the question.
0	Blank, completely inaccurate, inappropriate, or off topic.

Sample Response 1

The learning objectives for a one-week unit on the cell would include:

1. explain cell theory and describe the scientific contributions leading up to it,

2. know the structure and function of a cell's organelles,

3. describe and explain the structure and function of the cell membrane.

It is crucial for students to understand the cell theory, as stated in objective one because students need to understand that all living things - plants and animals - are made of cells and that these cells only come from preexisting cells. To illustrate science as a process, students should have knowledge of the scientific discoveries of Schwann, Virchow and others that lead to the cell theory. It is also important for students recognize that the cell is the basic unit of life. In being the basic unit of life, the cell must carry out various functions and processes. Through understanding structure and function of organelles, students can gain an understanding of how the cell can be a self-supporting unit. Also, students need to understand the structure and function of the cell membrane, as stated in objective three. It is the cell membrane that maintains homeostasis within the cell, and without such regulation a cell could die. Students should know the components of the cell membrane are phospholipids, proteins, carbohydrates and steroids and that these components do not have a fixed position, but rather than the positions of proteins, carbohydrates, and steroids can change with regard to their positions in the phospholipid bilayer.

To being this unit on the cell, one 45-minute session would be used acquainting students with the microscope. Students should become familiar with the parts of the microscope as well as with the way a microscope shows an image. A lab activity can be conducted using an "a" or an "e" from the newspaper to show students how a microscope shows the magnified image of an "e" upsidedown and reversed. Once students become familiar with the microscope, there can be a lecture on cell theory. A second 45-minute session could be spent on an activity with organelles. First the teacher would present a lecture about organelles, their structures and their functions. Afterwards, the students could break into groups of 4 or 5 and do further investigations of the organelles using other books or the Internet. Once the information is collected, students could compile a presentation comparing the cell to a city. Analogies could include comparing the mitochondria to a power plant and the nucleus to the city hall. A third 45 minute session could be used study the structure and function of the cell membrane. Through a brief lecture, students should learn that the cell membrane regulates what materials and substances enter and leave the cell. They also know the various components of the membrane, including phospholipids, proteins (integral and peripheral), carbohydrates and steroids. In addition to verbally explaining the composition of the cell membrane in lecture, the teacher could have the students build a cell membrane themselves. The media for the model can be such things as Jello or simply construction paper. For the construction paper model a set number of each component of the membrane is cut out of different colored construction paper and arranged accordingly. Yarn is used as the hydrocarbon tail of the phospholipid. One 90-minute session could be used investigating various cell structures such as the cell membrane, cell wall, chloroplasts and chromatin by observing slides of apple peel, apple pulp, onion peel and human cheek cells under the microscope. This would allow students to compare animal cells to plant cells. Protozoan cells can also be observed to give students comparison between prokaryotic and eukaryotic cells.

To assess student learning, various methods could be used. For example, the students could have a laboratory test during which they had to observe a cell under the microscope and determine whether it was prokaryotic or eukaryotic and if eukaryotic, whether it was plant or animal. Students would also list the structures on which they based their decision. For example, if a student observed a cell with a nucleus that contained chromatin, he would state that the cell was eukaryotic. If he also observed a cell wall and chloroplasts in that same cell, he would state that the cell was a plant cell and photosynthetic. This form of assessment would be used to evaluate whether students learned the structures of organelles as well as the types of cells. Specific organelles are found in plant versus animal, eukaryotic versus prokaryotic. This assessment will also be useful in determining if the student can correctly use the microscope. Therefore this assessment would be used to gage student understanding of objective one and two. An essay question could be used to gage student comprehension of objective three. Students could write an essay describing the structure of the cell membrane and explaining how the structure related to the function. An acceptable response would include that the cell membrane consists of a phospholipid bilayer with integral proteins and peripheral proteins. Students should also state that carbohydrates (away from the cytoplasm) and steroids (in animal cells) may be found in the membrane and that the position of these components is always changing as stated by the fluid mosaic model. A diagram of this model should be included in the students response that accurately depicts membrane structure. Also, students should include in their response that the membrane regulates what enters and leaves the cell by diffusion or protein-aided transport mechanisms (active and passive transport, etc.). Materials and substances that cannot dissolve in the phospholipid bilayer need assistance across the membrane, meaning that the cell membrane is selectively permeable or semipermeable. This idea that not all materials can cross the membrane is crucial to students' understanding of the membrane, and therefore should not be left out of their essay response.

Scores for Sample Response 1: total score of 10 (out of 15)

Part 1—3

Part 2—3

Part 3—4

Commentary on Sample Response 1

Part 1—The answer clearly indicates three acceptable objectives: cell theory, organelle structure and function, and membrane structure and function. Main ideas were stated for objectives 1 and 3 but not for objective 2. There was also a limited discussion of the importance of the objectives, especially as the cell unit relates to a biology course.

Part 2—Several key strategies are described in part 2. The development of microscope skills is fundamental to students' learning organelle structure-function and cell diversity, and it leads to student-led discovery exercises. Lecture and model building round out the test taker's strategies. While strategies for objectives 2 and 3 are fairly well detailed, there is little discussion of how understanding of cell theory will be achieved. In addition, the answer should elaborate on inquiry-based assignments related to microscopy.

Part 3—The answer concisely describes two end-of-unit, nonmultiple-choice assessment techniques that test students' understanding of all three objectives. Sample questions and expected student responses were provided. The use of each assessment tool was justified, but this area could have been developed more fully. Additionally, development of a rubric would have maximized the score in this section.

Sample Response 2

Students in a beginning biology class would be expected to gain a firm understanding of the cell theory, cellular structure and function, and cellular reproduction. In order to understand what a cell is, the student must know the cell theory including, all living things are composed of cells, cells are the smallest living unit, and all cells come from existing cells. In addition, to the cell theory itself, a brief historical account of the history of cell research and its prominent contributors may be called for. The work of Robert Hooke, for example, would be extremely relevant to the cell theory. If students understand the major components of the cell theory, the moving into the next objective of cellular structure and function will be more intuitive. Students would also learn the major distinctions between prokaryotic and eukaryotic cells. This will allow the student to be able to differentiate between plant, animal, and bacterial life, as well as where various organisms fall in respect to the five Kingdoms.

The second objective deals with cellular structure and function. A survey of organelles would be important so that students understand the "division of labor" and how the organelles help to carry out the various processes of respiration and replication. Students would need to learn about the structure and function of the phospholipid bilayer that exists, so that they can understand how cells retain some materials, while others move back and forth freely. This would call for a survey of various transport mechanisms, as well, including osmosis, diffusion, passive, and active transport and facilitated diffusion. Each type would be compared and contrasted to ensure a clear understanding of distinctions. Students would also need to be able to recognize all of the organelles by shape and understand their functions and inter-related functions. For example, the Golgi body "packages" materials to be sent to vesicles and enclosed for transport. Students would gain an understanding of respiration and energy production. Topics would include the Kreb's cycle, glycolysis, and oxidative phosphorylation. Distinctions between respiration and photosynthesis are also important because students will understand exactly why and how plants make their own food.

Cellular reproduction is an important concept because students need to understand the process of mitosis and meiosis as well as asexual reproduction such as fission and budding. The focus would be on the stages of mitosis and meiosis and how they contrast. Students would learn that mitosis occurs in somatic cells, while meiosis occurs in sex cells. Interphase → telophase, all stages would be discussed. Diseases and disorders in meiotic division would be discussed included sex-linked disorders and trisomy.

Lecture would be an invaluable tool (in combination with the text), for teaching the cell theory and its components. It would also help in teaching its history. Using models in conjunction with web based and software programs would allow students to see different organelles in action. Microscopy labs would allow students to see the difference cells. Modeling the mitotic and meiotic actions of cells would allow students to have a more kinestetic approach at cellular reproduction. Videos, diagrams, and software are also useful.

Students would be assessed on the first objective by a short essay question in which they must explain the cell theory and each of its components. The second objective would be assessed by a lab practical in which they must use microscopes to identify various structures including the nucleus and cell wall. They would also use microscopes to distinguish between animal and plant cells. Cell models would have various organelles flagged and students would have to identify the structures and explain their functions in as much detail as possible. The third objective could be assessed by either asking students to diagram mitosis/meiosis and explain in which type of cells they occur and list the various stages, or having students use pipe cleaners as models of chromosomes and allow them to model both mitosis and meiosis and explain, verbally, each stage as they progress.

The essay will assess a students knowledge of the cell theory and evaluate the depth of their understanding according to the detail of their response. The lab practical will evaluate a students ability to recognize cell parts and describe their function. Since the third objective could be evaluated in two different ways, this allows kinestetic learners to demonstrate their knowledge of mitosis and meiosis using a "hands-on" approach and allows students with different learning styles the opportunity to...... (response incomplete)

Scores for Sample 2: total score of 7 (out of 15)

    Part 1—4

    Part 2—1

    Part 3—2

Commentary on Sample Response 2

Part 1—Three distinct, comprehensive learning objectives were provided for part 1: cell theory, cell structure and function, and cellular reproduction. The answer gave a detailed description of main ideas and skills for the unit and provided generally clear rationales for the selection of each objective. To earn a score of 5 in this section, the answer would need to include a more detailed rationale and limit the extent of the content covered within each objective. It would be very unrealistic to try to cover that amount of material in a one-week unit.

Part 2—The response provided a list of strategies that were appropriate for the unit, but no strategy was described in suitable detail.

Part 3—The response provided descriptions of three assessment tools: an essay test, a lab practical, and modeling. All three objectives were assessed; however, the test taker gave only limited description of each assessment, the justification for its use, and information about how student mastery would be determined.

Sample Response 3

The student will be able to:

(1)   differentiate between a prokaryotic cell and a eukaryotic cell

(2)   differentiate between a plant and an animal cell

(3)   describe the functions of the major organelles found in plant and animal cells.

I feel as if I have chosen three broad objectives that are probably common in units on the cell. However, I do feel that each one is a significant step in developing this unit. To begin the unit students will need to learn what a cell is exactly and by explaining the difference between prokaryotic and eukaryotic cells you are beginning to differentiate between life forms, specifically between unicellular and multicellular organisms. Then you add another piece to the puzzle by having students become aware of cellular differences between multicellular organisms specifically plants and animals. Finally, the student can begin to think about how cells carry out the fundamentals of life such as respiration, metabolism, nutrient transport, etc. Each objective adds to the previous knowledge and stimulates students to critically think about and differentiate and apply each new piece of information.

To help students learn and be able to apply the content they will have:

Day 1: Objective One (45 mins) Laboratory investigations on day 1 which will contain slides of prokaryotes and eukaryotes organisms that will be placed in a drawing notebook (Any identifiable organelle will be drawn and labeled.) During direct instruction I will also show several slides of both prokaryotes and eukaryotes and talk about differences.

Day 2: Objective Two (45 mins) Students will work on an activity where they will label cellular organelles in a plant cell and an animal cell.

Day 3: Objective Three (45 mins) Laboratory investigation looking at several different types of plant and animals. Students will make drawing in their drawing notebooks.

Day 4: Objective Four (45 mins) Students will be asked to come up with an analogy that can be used to help them understand the functions of the major organelles.

EX   Cell is like a car
     nucleus = engine
     frame = plasma membrane
     windows = transport proteins
     etc.

*another good example is factory

Students will make a diagram using the analogy and give each student a copy of the diagram.

Day 5: Objectives 1, 2, 3 (90 mins) Students will discuss their analogy to the class and will take a lab practical.

Assessment:

Students will have a lab practical in which they have to identify certain organisms as prokaryotic and eukaryotic, plant or animal, etc. The lab practical will allow me to decide if students truly understood the difference between different types of cells and their physical appearance. The practical, however, will also have questions relating to each organisms that are from content material, for example, if a lab station is set up with a slide of onion root tip cells, the student may be asked to identify the type of cell (plant or animal) and also answer questions like, "Does this cell have small or large vacuoles?" "Does this cell have a cell wall?", etc. The drawing notebook and analogy diagram will also count as grades for this unit. I believe both of these could be valuable forms of assessment. By looking at them one could determine their understanding of content material. Both of these would be useful in deciding what needed to taught again.

Scores for Sample Response 3: total score of 6 (out of 15)

Part 1—2

Part 2—2

Part 3—2

Commentary on Sample Response 3

Part 1—The answer has indicated three acceptable objectives important to developing a comprehensive unit on the cell. The main ideas were very limited, and no skills were presented. The test taker should have presented enough information so that the scorers could determine whether the test taker was knowledgeable about key differences between prokaryotes and eukaryotes (e.g., the presence of a nucleus and membrane-bound organelles, cell size, metabolic differences, evolutionary trends), plants versus animals, organelle structure-function, and fundamental skills the students need (e.g., microscope technique). The response also provided a very limited rationale for the importance of these objectives in developing a cell unit.

Part 2—The response provided three strategies to help guide students: microscopic slide examination supported by direct instruction, a diagram-labeling activity, and student-developed analogies. While all three strategies are appropriate, the answer provided only limited descriptions of a few strategies, and the inquiry-based learning activities were not well developed.

Part 3—The first assessment tool, the lab practical, was rated as "fairly detailed" because specific slide types were identified and test questions regarding these slides were included. The second and third assessments, the drawing notebook and the analogy exercise, were integral to the test taker's instructional strategies and therefore were considered as ongoing assessment, not end-of-unit. The response failed to provide a clear and well-organized justification of their use as assessment tools and did not provide any specific information about student mastery (e.g., expected answers, a grading rubric).

Sample Response 4

A.   Objective: The student should learn the definition of a cell.
Objective: The student should learn the major difference between animal cells and plant cells.
Objective: The student should learn the various parts of the cell both plant and animal, and how they function.

It is important for them to learn the definition of the cell in order for them to achieve a basic understanding (familiarity) of what we are above to discuss in this unit. It is important for them to learn the major difference between plant and animal cell because these are the two forms of life that exist. It is also important that the students learn various parts of plant and animal cells and their function.

B. My instructional strategies would include lecture, video about plant and animal cells and their differences and functions of their organelles, a film, role play of each student as part of the cell and discussion. We would have a thorough review of cooperative learning.

C. One method of assessment that I would use would be a comprehensive written test. The test would include specific questions related only to the material that was covered. My second assessment would include a fun teachback on a report that each student was required to do. During this teachback the student will demonstrate everything that they learned about the cell in individual regard.

Scores for Sample Response 4: total score of 3 (out of 15)

Part 1—1

Part 2—1

Part 3—1

Commentary on Sample Response 4

Part 1—The answer has indicated only one acceptable objective. Stating the definition of the cell is not adequate by itself. Also, objectives 2 and 3 are overlapping. While an attempt to rationalize the objectives was made, the test taker only restated the objectives; no additional information was provided. The test taker did not discuss the importance of the objectives, the main ideas, or the skills students would be expected to learn.

Part 2—The answer only listed pedagogical strategies and did not explain how these strategies would specifically allow students to achieve the learning objectives. While there are many strategies common to education, relating them specifically to science and the unit are key in this section.

Part 3—Once again, the response provided only a list of nonspecific assessment tools. How these tools could test the knowledge and skills of students was not explained.

To Maximize Your Score on This Question

To maximize your score on part 1, be sure that the three objectives you choose are significant, and provide comprehensive coverage of the content domain. (Note that if three distinct objectives are not mentioned, your score for subsequent parts of the question will be affected adversely.) Be sure to provide clear, well-reasoned, and detailed explanations of the importance of these objectives within the cell unit. Also, consider how this unit is sequenced within a one-year biology course. How will this information relate to previously covered topics, and how will it help students understand the material yet to come? Finally, include a detailed description of main ideas and skills for each objective. You are being tested on your ability to develop meaningful content units. Demonstrating your knowledge of the content area is equally as important as developing creative and appropriate pedagogical strategies.

To maximize your score on part 2, make certain that several well-chosen strategies are fully detailed for each learning objective stated in part 1. These strategies should be engaging, be appropriate for a first-year high school course in biology, and use the 90-minute period adequately. Also, the timetable for completion of instruction should be realistic. Inquiry and laboratory-based instruction should be included.

To maximize your score on part 3, include fully detailed descriptions of two nonmultiple-choice, end-of-unit assessment methods that refer back to all three objectives from part 1. (Remember that true/false, matching, etc., are just modified versions of multiple-choice. These tools will not be given credit by scorers.) You must include a clear and well-organized justification for their use, as well as specific information about student mastery. Listing specific questions, expected answers, and a grading rubric is appropriate.

Physical Science: Pedagogy Test

The practice test question and a summary of the General Scoring Guide are restated below.

Question

Time—60 minutes

You are planning to teach a unit on radioactivity to a high school physical science class. Read the passage below and use the information to help you respond to parts 1, 2, 3, and 4 below.

> Radioactivity refers to the spontaneous transformation of an unstable atomic nucleus by the emission of radiation and/or particles. A specific transformation may occur within a time frame ranging from less than a microsecond to greater than billions of years. Each radioactive element has a particular mode, or modes, of decay, such as alpha, beta, and gamma decay.

1. Identify a major concept directly related to the topic of radioactivity as described in the paragraph above around which you will develop a lesson for a high school physical science class.

2. Describe the instructional strategies and classroom activities you would use to open, develop, and close this lesson. Include elements of inquiry-based learning in these strategies and activities. Explain why you think your strategies and activities would be appropriate and effective.

3. Describe in detail an appropriate assessment activity you would use in conjunction with this lesson. Explain why you think this activity would be appropriate and effective.

4. Identify and describe in detail a topic you would use for a follow-up lesson to build on this lesson. Explain why this topic would be appropriate and effective for a follow-up lesson.

NOTES

General Scoring Guide

Parts 1 and 2 combined, INSTRUCTIONAL STRATEGIES and ACTIVITIES, will be scored according to the following scoring rubric:

<u>Score</u>	<u>Comment</u>
5	Demonstrates a ***superior*** understanding of how to plan a physical science lesson, as evidenced by the following:

- shows evidence of a very good understanding of science content by using accurate language, graphs, equations, etc., appropriately in context with very good integration of concepts

- provides a fully detailed description of instructional strategies and activities that include elements of inquiry-based learning and are appropriate for teaching the lesson

- presents a lesson with a logical and definite structure

- provides a clear and logical explanation of why the instructional strategies and activities would be appropriate and effective

4	Demonstrates a ***strong*** understanding of how to plan a physical science lesson, as evidenced by the following:

- shows evidence of a good understanding of science content by using accurate language, graphs, equations, etc., appropriately in context

- describes in some detail instructional strategies and activities that include elements of inquiry-based learning and are appropriate for teaching the lesson

- presents a lesson with definite structure

- provides a brief but logical explanation of why the instructional strategies and activities would be appropriate and effective

3	Demonstrates an ***adequate*** understanding of how to plan a physical science lesson, as evidenced by the following:

- shows evidence of an adequate understanding of science content (including no major inaccuracies)

- provides a description of an instructional strategy and an activity that include elements of inquiry-based learning and are appropriate for teaching the lesson

- provides some evidence of structure in the lesson

- may or may **not** provide an explanation of why the instructional strategies and activities would be appropriate and effective

2   Demonstrates *limited* understanding of how to plan a physical science lesson, as evidenced by one or more of the following:

- shows evidence of a limited understanding of science content (possibly including major inaccuracies)

- provides a limited description of an instructional strategy or activity appropriate for teaching the lesson

- provides very limited evidence of structure in the lesson

1   Demonstrates *little or no* understanding of how to plan a physical science lesson, as evidenced by one or more of the following:

- shows evidence of poor understanding of science content

- may provide a vague or superficial description of an instructional strategy or activity appropriate for teaching the lesson

- provides no evidence of structure in the lesson

0   Completely inaccurate or inappropriate, blank, or off topic

Part 3, ASSESSMENT, will be scored according to the following scoring rubric:

Score	Comment

5   Demonstrates a *superior* understanding of how to plan an assessment activity, as evidenced by the following:

- provides a fully detailed description of an assessment activity appropriate for teaching the lesson

- provides a clear and logical explanation of why the assessment activity is appropriate and effective

4   Demonstrates a *strong* understanding of how to plan an assessment activity, as evidenced by the following:

- provides a detailed description of an assessment activity appropriate for teaching the lesson

- provides a logical explanation of why the assessment activity is appropriate and effective

3   Demonstrates an *adequate* understanding of how to plan an assessment activity, as evidenced by the following:

- provides a detailed description of an assessment activity appropriate for teaching the lesson

- may or may **not** provide an explanation of why the assessment activity is appropriate and effective

2   Demonstrates *limited* understanding of how to plan an assessment activity, as evidenced by the following:

- provides a limited description of an assessment activity appropriate for teaching the lesson

1   Demonstrates *little or no* understanding of how to plan an assessment activity, as evidenced by the following:

- may provide a vague or superficial description of an appropriate assessment activity related to the lesson

0   Completely inaccurate or inappropriate, blank, or off topic

Part 4, FOLLOW-UP, will be scored according to the following scoring rubric:

<u>Score</u>   <u>Comment</u>

5   Demonstrates a *superior* understanding of how to plan a follow-up lesson, as evidenced by the following:

- clearly identifies and provides a fully detailed description of a topic for a follow-up lesson appropriate to build on the first the lesson

- provides a clear and logical explanation of why the topic for the follow-up lesson is appropriate and effective

4   Demonstrates a *strong* understanding of how to plan a follow-up lesson, as evidenced by the following:

- clearly identifies and provides a detailed description of a topic for a follow-up lesson appropriate to build on the first lesson

- provides a logical explanation of why the topic for the follow-up lesson is appropriate and effective

3   Demonstrates an *adequate* understanding of how to plan a follow-up lesson, as evidenced by the following:

- identifies and provides a description of a topic for a follow-up lesson appropriate to build on the first lesson

- may or may **not** provide an explanation of why the follow-up lesson is appropriate and effective

2   Demonstrates *limited* understanding of how to plan a follow-up lesson, as evidenced by the following:

- provides a limited description of a topic for a follow-up lesson appropriate to build on the first lesson

1   Demonstrates *little or no* understanding of how to plan a follow-up lesson, as evidenced by the following:

- provides a vague or superficial description of a topic for a follow-up lesson related to the first lesson

0   Completely inaccurate or inappropriate, blank, or off topic

Sample Response 1

1. I would develop my lesson around 1/2-lives and their function in aiding the dating of fossil material. It will help contruct a timeline for natural history.

2. a   The lesson would open with a discussion of dinosaurs. We would discuss when they were alive. The class would be led to the conclusion that were no humans around to record when they were alive; "so how do we know."

    b. From here we would discuss different means of dating things (ie gray hair on people, rings in a tree, etc). "Are these absolute or relative ages?" Then we would discuss the ways of dating rocks. We would briefly discuss the Law of Superposition as a relative age and radioactive 1/2-lives as an absolute age.

    c. From here we would "shift gears". We would have a brief math discussion → what is 1/2 of 2; what is 1/2 of 8; 1/2 of 100 etc. Next I would use this to demonstrate how a 1/2 life is used to date fossils. "If a rock has 64 grams of radioactive element in it today & its 1/2 life is 1 day; how many grams of r-a. element will it have tomorrow? (answer) What has happened to the other 32 grams → it has become 32 grams of decay material. If we wait another day, how much r-a. material do we have (16g) and how much decay? 48 → 32 + 16 or 64-16 From there we would discuss using ratios & fractions to determine how many 1/2 lives hare passed

ratio radio active: decay + total # of 1/2 live

1:1 → 0

1:2 → 1

1:4 → 2 $1:2^n$ n= # of 1/2 lives

1:8 → 3

1:16 → 4

Fraction radioactive element/total r.a. element + decay element

$1/2^n$ = # of 1/2 lives

d. the lesson would be closed with some time for practice solving problems for 1/2-lives. This would be followed by a wrap up showing how this has been used to date the Earth.

e. An activity to demonstrate 1/2 life would be the "pennies in a box" experiment. 1st put 50 pennies in a box →all heads up. 2nd shake the box for 30 seconds→ take out all tails up. Pennies: Should be approx. 25. Call this 1 1/2 life. 3rd replace the lid and shake again for 30 sec → call this 1/2-life #2. 4th remove tails up pennies should be approx. 12-13. Repeat again.

E. I believe that this lesson is appropriate because it shows the concept of 1/2 life very well. The math that is involved is fairly simple & a high-school student should be able to master it. The "Pennies" example gives a visible example of 1/2 lives for the visual learners in the classroom. It can also be "hands on" for those children who need that.

3. A 1/2 life worksheet could be generated to test their understanding. It would have some basic definitions as well as some mathematical manipulations on it. They would be effective b/c it would give the students a chance to show mastery of the subject. It would show who had mastered & who had not. they would open the door for some "peer tutoring" within the classroom. This worksheet would show me areas that were needed to be reviewed the most before an exam on the entire unit was to be given.

4. as a follow-up to this lesson, I would discuss why being able to put an absolute age on something is better than a relative age. This could lead to a discussion of "Faulting" and what that can do to layers of the Earth. I would give the specific example of a "Thrust Fault" and how is deposits older rock on top of younger rock. So if you base your dating only on the Law of Superposition, you will get faulty data.

This would be appropriate & effective b/c it ties the previous lesson of Radioactive dating in with the next topic of Plate Tectonics & Earthquakes.

3. Some sample math Problems from the worksheet could be

1a. if you have 1g of r-a-element & 1 gram of decay element, how many 1/2-lives has it undergone?

1 ra + 1 decay = 2 total

r-a/total = 1/2 = $1/2^n$ n = 1 1/2 life

1b If the 1/2 life = 1000 years how many years has it been since this rock was formed?

11/2 life. 1000 years = 1000 years

2. If the ratio of r-a material to decay material is 1:15 how many 1/2 lives have passed

total = r-a + decay = 1 + 15 = 16

ratio r-a: total = 1:16 = $1:2^n$ n = # of 1/2 lives

$16 = 2^n$

n = 3 1/2 lives

b. if the 1/2 life is $.\overline{3333}$ billion years, how many years has it been since the rock was formed?

$3*.\overline{33}$ billion years = 1 billion years

etc.

Scores for Sample Response 1: total score of 16 (out of 20)
(scores from parts 1 and 2 combined are doubled)

Parts 1 and 2—4

Part 3—4

Part 4—4

Commentary on Sample Response 1

Part 1—The response directly addresses the question and describes the topic as centering on the concept of half-life. The test taker continues on topic by mentioning fossil dating and constructing a timeline for natural history.

Part 2—*Content.* The response presents a very good understanding of science content as described in the General Scoring Guide, for example, using the Law of Superposition as an indicator of relative age and half-life as a means of measuring age in an absolute sense; the change radioactive materials undergo to become decay materials; and the specific example using simple numbers and formulas ($1:2^n$, where n = # of half-lives).

Lesson Structure. The response presents a lesson with detail. The detail includes a short introduction by the teacher and then focuses on the details involved in the determination and meaning of half-life. The reference to closing the lesson with some time to practice problem solving is generic and weakens the description. The activity described in part E could have been integrated more smoothly into the entire lesson. A weakness in the activity is that it removes the pennies rather than replacing them with other more stable "atoms" (possibly dimes).

Appropriate and Effective Statement. The last paragraph justifies the lesson in terms of accuracy and meeting the needs of high school students.

Part 3—The assessment for this lesson is a work sheet involving more half-life problems and definitions. The strength of this response lies in the purpose of the work sheet. A further strength in the assessment lies in the fact that the students will be better prepared to score well in the upcoming unit test. Due to the brevity of the response, the scorers lowered the score. The writer does include a few specific example problems for the work sheet at the end of the essay. The general approach seems disorganized, but this did not enter into the scoring. The scorers looked for every opportunity to award the test taker the maximum possible score based on the scoring guide. This serves as a good example of a response that satisfies many of the points from the General Scoring Guide. The added page of sample problems for the work sheet probably raised the score from a 3 to the final score of 4.

Part 4—The test taker used a comparison of the absolute dating used in radioactivity studies and the relative dating of rocks using the Law of Superposition. The follow-up lesson is shorter and less detailed than the original lesson, but that is to be expected. There is good evidence that the test taker understands the content (uses a diagram to highlight Superposition) and related concepts (Thrust Fault). There is an important link to the concept of the original lesson, and the link is logical. Finally, the test taker includes a rationale as to why the follow-up is appropriate and effective. The follow-up was not fully described, but it did identify the topic and provide some details.

Sample Response 2

> 1. In a middle school classroom, I would talk about radioactivity. I would define it, describe how it was found, and what measures radioactivity in substances now.
>
> 2. I would open the class by asking them if they know what radioactivity is. I would proceed with a mini lesson on radioactivity, which would last about ten minutes. It is better to lecture students as little as possible, and give the majority of classroom time to hands-on/mind-on activities. Students will retain more information about science if they are allowed to experience sciences. During the mini-lesson radioactivity would be defined. I would ask

the students to write a definition of radioactivity in their science notebooks that is in their own words. If students can take information and put in a way that they understand, the student will remember the definition of radioactivity, and the student will learn the definition of the topic or concept. After they have written their definition in their notebook, I would ask if they know how radioactivity was discovered. I would then explain how Marie Curie discovered radioactivity by accident in her lab. Then I would ask students to brainstorm about what type of materials are radioactivity. This is a way to measure student's prior knowledge of the object. This is also a way to get students thinking about the topic, and hopefully, get the students interested in finding out what materials are really radioactive. After we have brainstormed, I would say that we were going to test their predictions of radioactivity materials with a classroom activity called "What is Radioactive" The students will get into lab groups. It is good for students to work in groups, because it enhances their social skills and cooperation skills. In groups students will test objects and materials with a guger counter to measure the radioactivity in each thing tested. After students have tested their objects and measured the amount of radioactivity in each with the geiger counter, the students will again be brought back to a whole class setting. I would ask for results of the objects. In this, students can compare their findings with other students. If their are differences such as certain objects/materials have more radioactive materials in them than others. In closing, I would ask them to tell me what the definition of radioactivity was again. I would do this so the concept is addressed. This is also a way for me to check for understanding and to make sure the definition they wrote in their science journal was correct.

3. an assessment activity that could be used with this lesson is to have students write a scientific journal about their findings in the activity that was completed in the lesson. It is important for teachers to help improve students writing skills throughout all content areas. In this journal, the students would have to define radioactivity, give background for it such as how it was discovered, techniques used to measure it, and explain the activity thoroughly. They will have to explain the results in words and with a graph on chart. This activity would be a good review of the lesson above and it would allow the teacher to check for understanding. It would also

allow students to develop the science process skill of reading charts and graphs.

4. For a follow-up lesson, I would describe the types of rays that are given off with radioactivity. I would use the teaching method of jigsaw to do this, because this was students will be reading about a topic. Students would be broken up in groups of three. One person from each group would go to a table with materials about either alpha, beta, or gamma rays. The student would become the expert for their group about the type of rays, then they would go back to their group and teach the group about their ray. The groups would have a chart to fill in about each type of ray. After every group has had time to fill in the chart, I would go over the charts to make sure they have completed them. Then I would discuss how these rays affect us in our everyday life. It is important for students to understand how these topics affect us in real-life and not just in a lab. This helps bring a new meaning of science to them. This would be a good follow-up lesson because it expands on radioactivity and it relates it to real life.

Scores for Sample Response 2: total score of 12 (out of 20)
(scores from parts 1 and 2 combined are doubled)

Parts 1 and 2—3

Part 3—2

Part 4—4

Commentary on Sample Response 2

Part 1—The response clearly identifies a topic related to the prompt around which to develop a lesson.

Part 2—The response gives evidence of good organization of the lesson. There is an opening activity, the minilesson. The comment that students are better served when given hands-on activities is used to justify the use of the minilesson to present ideas. The score of 3 is assigned since the response shows evidence of good structure in the lesson, even though the science content was not a strong point.

Part 3—A journal entry was used as an assessment. There was not enough detail in the assessment. After a good start, the test taker seems to miss points here.

Part 4—The test taker uses a jigsaw technique in describing the follow-up lesson. This technique is well developed. A justification for the follow-up is present.

Sample Response 3

1. I would use the major concepts of disposal of radioactive materials to develop a lesson for a high school physical science class. Recently Nevada, where I plan to teach, has been designated as a holding site for radioactive waste material. This material is the by-product of nuclear power plants.

I would focus on the time frames for those specific transformations modes of decay. I would use a current magazine or newspaper article to gain students attention. Then with the article introduce the possible impact of storing radioactive material in Nevada.

The students would understand that the storage of material is a long term commetment. This commetment comes with environmental consequences and containment facility obligations.

Once the material is in Nevada, we must be willing to deal with its hazardous properties for our lifetimes.

2. I would open this lesson with flim clips from the nuclear accidents at three mile island in the U.S. and the accident at chernoble in Russia. I would high light the environmental impacts the alpha, gamma, and beta particles had on the surrounding areas of these two accident.

To develop the lesson, I would have students do a computer simulation. I would introduce and demonstrate the simulation by using a radioactive element that was use at threemile Island and show how long it would take for this elements hazardous properties to decay.

At the completion of this demonstration, I would distribute the students into group of two and assign them to their computers. Each group would have a study guide to help them accomplish the programed lesson on the computer. The computer simulation would guide the student through the concepts of Radio active decay for gamma, alpha and beta particles. Each student would complete a correlated programed worksheet based upon the computer simulation

I would close the lesson by having the students return to their individual desks and write a Journel entry about the facility they would construct to contain the decaying nuclear emission.

My lesson would work because I related it to historical events the students have studied in other classes. I also related the lesson to their state of residence and local area. I would have their attention.

Using a guided lesson stradegy would work well to allow each student to explore how different types of radioactive materials decay. This would let him or her experience the problem of finding a nuclear fuel that has a limited half life for use as a fuel.

Finally, closing with a Journel entry lets the student try to solve the obvious problem of containing these fuels after use they would be interested in persuving their hometown environment.

3. The assessment activity would be programed work sheet that was correlated with the computer simulation. The worksheet would ask questions that the student could answer by using the simulation. For example, the simulation would begin by having a student examine different radioactive materials for use as fuel in a power plant. The student would learn that some fuel work well as a fuel and some do not.

Next the simulation would guide the student through the types of emission produced and their associated half lives. The student then would have to use the simulation to answer questions about the half lifes of fuel emission that our usually used in power plants.

The other assessment used would be the Journel entry. I would be able to correlate and establish what the student understands about containing these emission and apply that information to a follow on lesson concerning the safe storage of decaying radio active material.

4. As a follow up lesson, I would present the appropriate methods for storage of decaying radioactive material. This lesson would present the properties of alpha, gamma, and beta particles and why they require special storage considerations. This lesson would work well with the previous lesson because it will provide the answers to the journal entry the students had made the day/lesson before.

Scores for Sample Response 3: total score of 12 (out of 20)
(Scores from parts 1 and 2 combined are doubled.)

Parts 1 and 2—3

Part 3—3

Part 4—3

Commentary on Sample Response 3

Part 1—The response describes the topic to be discussed as that of disposal of radioactive waste. The test taker explains that the concept of radioactive waste disposal is a topic of particular interest for students in Nevada, where the test taker plans to teach. This comment effectively justifies using the topic. Although the test taker has labeled this as part 1, there are a number of components of part 2 incorporated into this part of the response. Although the response is somewhat disorganized, the scorers give credit to the test taker for these ideas. The spelling errors would be considered minor errors and would not affect the score.

Part 2—The lesson uses a multimedia presentation. The test taker plans to use a video clip of various nuclear accidents and a computer simulation. There are two dangers in this approach: First, it avoids specific content. The scorers are left to assume that the content in the chosen videotape and simulation is accurate. Thus, the test taker fails to give evidence of good or very good understanding of science content. Second, the test taker does not actually design the lesson. In a sense, it is the modern form of the "plan in a can" of a generation ago. Generally, computer simulations are good for presenting concepts. The test taker describes the program as a guided trip through content dealing with alpha, beta, and gamma radiation. Toward the end of the lesson, the test taker indicates that the computer program would let students experience the problem of finding a nuclear fuel that has a limited half-life. This would introduce some elements of inquiry, but this does not seem to be a major focus of the lesson. The lesson does have structure, with an opening, development, and a closing. This would be considered a strength in the lesson. The test taker includes a justification for the appropriateness of the lesson.

The response shows a satisfactory structure and rationale for why the lesson should work. However, to merit a 4 or 5, the response needs both more detailed content and increased use of inquiry elements.

Part 3—The test taker states that the assessment will involve the use of a programmed work sheet that would accompany the computer simulation. A strength of this approach is that a strong link to the original lesson is obvious. The weakness is that the test taker loses an opportunity to demonstrate creativity in the assessment. The test taker also includes a journal entry as part of the assessment. According to the test taker, the journal entry will establish what the students understand about "containing these emissions." The test taker is using the assessment as a means of preparing students for the follow-up lesson. This dual purpose for the assessment provides a strong rationale for its appropriateness and effectiveness.

Part 4—The follow-up lesson deals with methods for storing decaying radioactive material. The follow-up lesson makes an excellent link with the original lesson as well as with the assessment. One weakness is that the length of the follow-up is short. The scorers assigned a score of 3 because of the quality of the unit presentation and the overall linkage. There is a strong flow from one lesson to the next. The short length prevented a score of 4 or 5.

Sample Response 4

1. At the beginning of class I would do a brief summary of yesterdays topic. Then I would use an inductive approach to teach that days lesson on the Degeneration of matter.

   Lesson Plan (Radioactivity)
   1. review yesterdays highlight
   2. state my objectives
      A. Teach class What is the Decay of matter by using an inductive approach.
      B. Relate it to past lesson s
   3. Do a demonstrations (degeneration of materials)
   4. Teach information to class
   5. Apply what we learned with a hands on lab
   6. Review what we learned
   7. Assign homework (research and find the answer for 10 elements and their radioactivity)

2. A review of yesterdays topic would be my first step. Next, I would inform them about what we are going to learn today (decay of matter). I would open the lesson today with a demonstration about the decay of matter. I would show how different materials have depleted over time. The next thing to do after the hands on demo is to leave them with two questions. Why do things decay? And do all thing decay at the same rate. I would then proceed into my lecture-discussion session. In this session I would inform them what radioactivity is where it comes from and how long it takes for different materials to decay. I would strongly encourage their partisipation in our discussion. After our lecture-discussion session is over I would do a lab to show them some examples of how matter has decayed. I would then have them to do a lab write up on what they observed and draw conclusions. At the end of class I would have everyone go back to their seat so I could summarize what we have learn. I also would inform them to write in their Journal section of their notebook two things that I have learned today.

   The last thing form the class period is to assign homework. For that night it would be to do research on ten different elements. Each student should find out how long the half-life is for those elements. They will be due the next day in class.

I believe this will be effective because you need to get the students involved in your lesson. If they are asking questions and answering questions the usally they are paying attention and LEARNING. Involvement is the Key.

3. The next day when they come to class. I would give them five short answer questions regarding the previous days lesson. I do this everyday in my classes because I feel as though it helps them to remember what they did the day before. Of course after all the material for that section is completed we would have an overall test.

4. My follow-up lesson would be on the different modes of decay, alpha, beta and gamma. I feel this would lead to a greater understanding of that students comprehension of radioactivity. It would be appropriate because the students are learning more information on radioactivity and its different modes.

Scores for Sample Response 4: total score of 8 (out of 20)
(Scores from parts 1 and 2 combined are doubled.)

Parts 1 and 2—2

Part 3—2

Part 4—2

Commentary on Sample Response 4

Part 1—No topic is identified. This prevents a clear focus for the development of the lesson.

Part 2—The answer shows limited evidence of understanding of science content. The structure of the lesson shows some merit, and there is evidence that the test taker understands that encouraging class participation will enhance student learning. There are some concerns as to the safety of the lab exercise mentioned in the response. Having students handle radioactive materials in the lab is potentially dangerous.

Part 3—The assessment involves five questions from the previous lesson, but there are no specific examples of what kinds of questions might be appropriate. Since the lesson itself is vague, the assessment was limited and brief. The brevity is an obvious factor in this response.

Part 4—This follow-up lesson is very brief, although it does have a direct link to the original lesson. It also uses language directly from the prompt. With no original ideas in the response, the scorers cannot assume that the test taker is competent. In addition, the test taker took some time to sketch out a lesson plan (as part of part 1). Although it may have seemed like a good approach to responding to this part of the question, it did require time. This loss of time may have affected the test taker's ability to respond fully to parts 3 and 4.

Now that you've seen a sample question, test takers' responses, and the scorers' evaluation of the responses—it's time to practice. You are given one hour to complete your response to the *Life Science: Pedagogy* question or the *Physical Science: Pedagogy* question. While there are many versions of the question, in general the question's components are always very similar. It is the topic that changes. With that in mind, first practice writing a response to "The Cell" or "Radioactivity" question. How does your answer compare to the General Scoring Guide rubrics or to the other test takers' responses? How will you improve it to earn a score of 4 or 5 on each part? Next, think of other major instructional units that would be appropriate for a first-year high school biology, chemistry, or physics course. Write and evaluate your responses. Practice of this kind is likely to improve your chances of success on the test.

Chapter 11

Are You Ready? Last-Minute Suggestions

▶ ▶ ▶ ▶ ▶ ▶ ▶ ▶ ▶ ▶ ▶ ▶

Checklist

❑ Do you know the testing requirements for your teaching field in the state(s) where you plan to teach?

❑ Have you followed all of the test registration procedures?

❑ Do you know the topics that will be covered in each test you plan to take?

❑ Have you reviewed any textbooks, class notes, and course readings that relate to the topics covered?

❑ Do you know how long the test will take and the number of questions it contains? Have you considered how you will pace your work?

❑ Are you familiar with the test directions and the types of questions for the test?

❑ Are you familiar with the recommended test-taking strategies and tips?

❑ Have you practiced by working through the practice test questions at a pace similar to that of an actual test?

❑ If you are repeating a Praxis Series™ Assessment, have you analyzed your previous score report to determine areas where additional study and test preparation could be useful?

The Day of the Test

You should have ended your review a day or two before the actual test date. And many clichés you may have heard about the day of the test are true. You should

■ Be well rested.

■ Take photo identification with you.

■ Take blue or black ink pens for this constructed-response test.

■ Take your admission ticket, letter of authorization, mailgram or telegram with you.

■ Eat before you take the test, and take some food or a snack to keep your energy level up.

- Wear layered clothing; room temperature may vary.

- Be prepared to stand in line to check in or to wait while other test takers are being checked in.

You can't control the testing situation, but you can control yourself. Stay calm. The supervisors are well trained and make every effort to provide uniform testing conditions, but don't let it bother you if the test doesn't start exactly on time. You will have the necessary amount of time once it does start.

You can think of preparing for this test as training for an athletic event. Once you've trained, and prepared, and rested, give it everything you've got. Good luck.

Appendix A
Study Plan Sheet

▶ ▶ ▶ ▶ ▶ ▶ ▶ ▶ ▶ ▶ ▶ ▶

Study Plan Sheet

See Chapter 1 for suggestions on using this Study Plan Sheet.

STUDY PLAN						
Content covered on test	How well do I know the content?	What material do I have for studying this content?	What material do I need for studying this content?	Where could I find the materials I need?	Dates planned for study of content	Dates completed

Appendix B

For More Information

Educational Testing Service offers additional information to assist you in preparing for The Praxis Series™ Assessments. *Tests at a Glance* booklets and the *Registration Bulletin* are both available without charge (see below to order). You can also obtain more information from our Web site: **www.ets.org/praxis/index.html.**

General Inquiries

Phone: 609-771-7395 (Monday-Friday, 8:00 A.M. to 8:00 P.M., Eastern time)
Fax: 609-771-7906

Extended Time

If you have a learning disability or if English is not your primary language, you can apply to be given more time to take your test. The *Registration Bulletin* tells you how you can qualify for extended time.

Disability Services

Phone: 609-771-7780
Fax: 609-771-7906
TTY (for deaf or hard-of-hearing callers): 609-771-7714

Mailing Address

Teaching and Learning Division
Educational Testing Service
P.O. Box 6051
Princeton, NJ 08541-6051

Overnight Delivery Address

Teaching and Learning Division
Educational Testing Service
Distribution Center
225 Phillips Blvd.
P.O. Box 77435
Ewing, NJ 08628-7435